AMWELL AND STANSTEAD'S
PAST IN PICTURES

Other publications by Stephen Doree

Domesday Book and the Origin of Edmonton Hundred
Edmonton Hundred Historical Society, 1986

(Editor) *The Parish Register and Tithing Book of Thomas Hassall of Amwell*
Hertfordshire Record Society, 1989

A Short History of Trent Park
Middlesex Polytechnic, 1990

(Editor) *Early Churchwardens' Accounts of Bishops Stortford 1431–1558*
Hertfordshire Record Society, 1994

Other publications by David Perman

Cublington: A Blueprint for Resistance
Bodley Head, 1973

Change and the Churches
Bodley Head, 1977

(Editor) *A Quaint Old-Fashioned Place: East Hertfordshire in the 1830s*
Hertfordshire Publications, 1990

600 Years of Charity: A Brief History of the Ware Charity Trustees
Ware Museum, 1991

A New Guide to Scott's Grotto
Ware Society, 1991

Ware's Past in Pictures (with Maurice Edwards)
Rockingham Press, 1991

(Editor) *Ware in Poems and Prints*
Ware Museum, 1992

A Walk About Ware Guide (with John Fletcher)
Ware Society, 1995

AMWELL AND STANSTEAD'S PAST IN PICTURES

by

Stephen Doree
and David Perman

The Rockingham Press

First published 1997
by The Rockingham Press
11 Musley Lane,
Ware, Herts SG12 7EN

A catalogue record for this book is available
from the British Library

ISBN 1 873468 57 1

Printed in Great Britain by
Biddles Limited
Guildford

In memory of
Edward ("Ted") Chandler
1931-1996

ACKNOWLEDGEMENTS

We are grateful to the National Monuments Record Centre and to the editor of the *Hertfordshire Mercury* for permission to publish the photographs which are identified as their copyright in the captions. We must also express our thanks for the loan of photogaphs to Dr. Kate Thompson, Hertfordshire County Archivist, to Christine Shearman, Hertfordshire Local Studies Librarian, to Dr. Rosemary Bennett and Margaret Harris of the Hertford Museum, to Neil Robbins, Curator of Lowewood Museum, Hoddesdon, to the Trustees of the Ware Museum and to Russ Craig of the Hertfordshire Building Preservation Trust (BEAMS). Thanks are also due to the Council and Governors of Haileybury for access to the college archives.

Among the many people who have lent their collections of old postcards and photographs, special mention must be made of Gwen Chandler, Sam and Jim Newman, Tim Chaplin, David Dent, Len Kiff and the Great Amwell Women's Institute. Gwen Chandler gave us unrestricted access to the large archive of photographic material relating to Stanstead Abbotts which she collected with her late husband Ted, who should have been the author of this book, and to whose memory the book is dedicated. Sam and Jim Newman provided not merely a large number of illustrations, but also shared their memories of Stanstead Abbotts over a period (in Jim's case) of over 70 years, and were unstinting in their help and enthusiasm. Many of the Newmans' photographs are copies of originals long since lost made by their nephew, the photographer Paul Damen (telephone/fax: 01263 720973) who kindly allowed us to use them. The albums of the Chaplin family, kindly lent by Tim Chaplin, and of the Great Amwell Women's Institute provided fascinating photographic documentation of Great Amwell over more than a century, and we are grateful to Kay Todd and the other officers of the Great Amwell Women's Institute for the use of their material. A special word of thanks is also due to Mrs Elizabeth ('Betty') Sewell, the recent custodian of the album, for her enthusiasm and hospitality. To Len Kiff is due a special tribute: without the topographical foundation provided by his collection of high quality illustrations, the inclusion of Hertford Heath in this book might have been in doubt. David Dent has also been unfailingly generous in making available a large number of his superb illustrations.

We must record also our gratitude to a host of friends who have lent us photographs, provided valuable background information or helped in ways too numerous to mention, especially the following: Roger Alexander of Messrs Electrotest, Margaret Ball, Lily Bean, Ron Berry, Mike Bishop, A.T. Bridgeman, Ivy Burt, Vikky Burt, Frank Chappell, Elizabeth and Douglas Coakley, Nigel Copping, Lynda Cowler, Ken and John Cutler, Sidney Erskine-Murray, Doris Field, Harry and Gwen Fitch, the Revd. Dr. Barrie Goodwin and Sheila Baldock for allowing us to use material from the St. Margaret's Church Book, Helen and Andrew Hambling, Dorothy Hindlaugh, Guy Horlock of Messrs French and Jupp's, Sally Howard, Rosemary Imroth, Peter King, Derek Kitteringham, Iris Lyon, Alastair Macpherson, Mary and Tom Miller, Esme and Gerald Nix, Catherine Perry, Ruth Swallow, Lynda Thompson, Anthony and Joan Trower, the Revd. Edward and Jean Walker, and Bob and Pam Wilkins. We wish to thank all the peoples of these villages who willingly cooperated with two outsiders to make this work such a pleasure.

We must also acknowledge two further special debts — to Mrs C.M. (Mollie) Matthews, whose *Haileybury since Roman Times* is among the best researched of local histories; and to the pupils and teachers of St. Andrew's school, Stanstead Abbotts, who in 1949 conducted a valuable survey of their village. In a foreword, a young contributor wrote: "Maybe in 50 years' time someone interested in the growth of the village may consult its pages for information." That hope has been realised in this book.

CONTENTS

In Terram Meam

Happy are they whose hearts and hopes lie deep,
    Fast rooted in this fair and homely shire;
Maybe some travel far, yet ever keep
    Sweet memories to which their minds retire.

For some it is the county of their birth,
    The place in which they happily were born;
Hence, 'tis to them the dearest spot on earth,
    The place to which their love and longings turn.

For others, 'tis the county of their choice,
    Drawn by the wooing of its hills and streams;
The love of later years finding a voice:
    'This is the country of my early dreams'.

Happy are we who call this shire our home,
    Land of our birth or of our later love;
If 'tis our lot in distant fields to roam,
    We homeward turn, like Noah's returning dove.

A.J. Treloar
Vicar of Stanstead Abbotts 1927-32

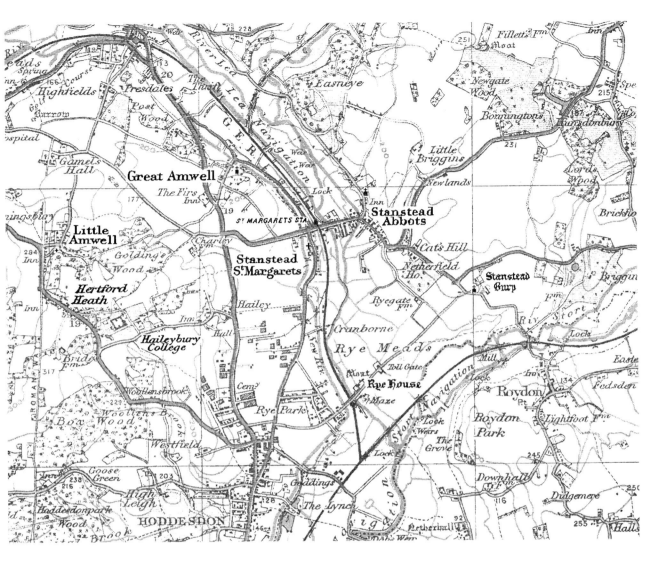

The four parishes from a tourist map of 1915

INTRODUCTION

Great Amwell, St. Margarets and Stanstead Abbotts are distinct parishes, each with its own historical traditions; they share a common access to the River Lea. Hertford Heath stands apart, though for the great part of its recorded history most of it lay within the parish of Great Amwell. Little Amwell, which is now part of the recently-formed parish of Hertford Heath, was for centuries a hamlet within the parish of All Saints Hertford before being formed into its own ecclesiastical district in 1863. Until the late 19th century, Little Amwell enjoyed its own independent access to the River Lea and was celebrated because it contained within its bounds Chadwell Spring, the source of the New River.

The purpose of this book is to present a visual record of the recent past of these communities. It is not our intention to present their separate and largely unwritten histories, but some historical discussion has been necessary to make these pictures and their interpretation intelligible.

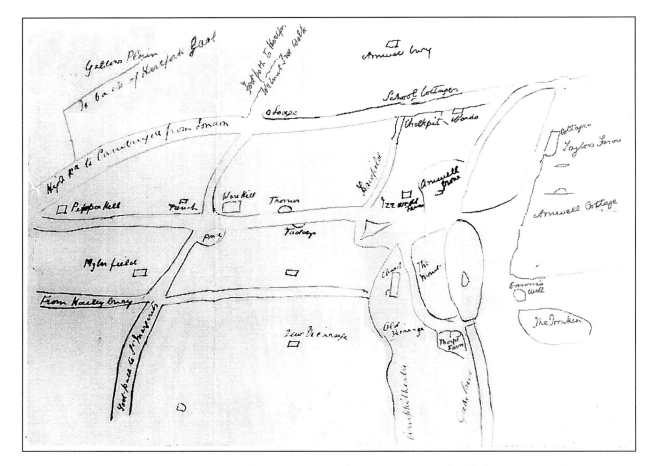

A sketch-map of Great Amwell village, originally drawn in 1818 and added to in the early 1840s when Great Amwell was undergoing upheaval just after the enclosure of the common fields.

West is at the top where Walnut Tree Walk runs off the map. Below that and running from left to right is the Hoddesdon-Ware road (now the A1170). Linking the main road with the Pool and the New River — the most prominent features on this map — is Cautherley Lane, named in the 20th century after a resident of Pepper Hill House shown on the left. In the centre of Cautherley Lane is Ware Hill House (now known as Great Amwell House) which was named after the contemporary Major John Ware, who also gave his name to Madgeways (Major Ware's) Lane. Farther along Cautherley Lane widens out to form a small green around the Quart Pot alehouse (now the George The Fourth) at the heart of the village. Close by are the church, Thorpe's Farm (now River Cottage), The Mount and Izzard's Farm (now gone). On the right are Taylor's (now Sheepcote) Farm and Amwell Cottage (now Well House). Below them is Emma's Well.

The original map was amended after 1840 when the 'New Vicarage' was built. But this must have been before 1845 when William Chadwell Mylne moved Hodson's 'Turret' to the garden of Home Lodge (the unnamed house just above the new vicarage). The Amphitheatre, an ancient earthwork shown below the 'Old Vicarage', was demolished in the 1860s.

Altogether, though roughly drawn, the map is an important historical record.

Great Amwell from the air in 1968. The original village clustered around the church and is largely buried beneath the New River of 1613 and the landscaping of the 19th century country houses. Great Amwell House (formerly Ware Hill) is in the lower foreground; Glebe House is at the right edge, the 'Old' Vicarage of 1840 nearer the top.

GREAT AMWELL:
AROUND THE VILLAGE

The parish of Great Amwell, which at one time included part of Hoddesdon town and Amwell End in Ware, has the village at its centre. This has has three focal points: the ancient church, the village centre and Amwell Pool.

The Church of St. John the Baptist, situated on a steep bank, commands a view of the Lea Valley and was originally, with the now-destroyed ancient encampment above it, part of an early defensive arrangement. The village centre, just outside the gates of the churchyard, was re-modelled in the late 19th century to create a three-piece village 'stage-set' consisting of the George the Fourth public house, The Mount and Filmer Cottage.

Amwell Pool was landscaped in the later 1790s by Robert Mylne, chief engineer to the New River Company. Intended originally simply to honour Sir Hugh Myddelton, creator of the New River in the years 1609-13, the Pool was to confer on Amwell the image with which it was to be henceforth identified by Victorian writers and illustrators.

Above: *A panoramic view of Great Amwell looking north-west from the church, commissioned in 1869 by John Cussans for his* History of Hertfordshire. *Cussans commented: 'Ware in the background. Railroad is behind the line of trees. Footpath by the side of the New River appears as a white patch. Footpath by the side of the New River from St. Margarets. It joins the bye-road which leads from Amwell to the Hertford High Road'.*
Below: *St. John's Lane, Great Amwell, in about 1905. On the right are the now-demolished church cottages of 1859. On the left (out of the picture behind the white fence) are the almshouses*

Above: *The village centre of Great Amwell in the 1890s had an image that was both traditional and 'polite'. The traditional elements in this scene were the George the Fourth public house (once the Quart Pot alehouse) in the centre, and Izzard's Farm (long vanished) down the hill to its left; the 'polite' elements were The Mount, Robert Mylne's early 19th century house, and Filmer's Cottage on the right re-designed by his grandson in 1887 in honour of Queen Victoria's Golden Jubilee.*

Below: *The same village centre of Great Amwell in 1905 was wholly 'polite' after the George the Fourth received its facelift in the 1890s. The balance of the landscape composition was later marred when The Mount burned down and the top storey was not rebuilt.*

Great Amwell, Herts.

Left: *On the larger of the two New River islands is the Memorial, erected by Robert Mylne in 1800 as a tribute to Sir Hugh Myddelton who constructed the New River in the years 1609-13.*

Right: *Part of a 1905 postcard of the other island and the stone, on which is engraved Archdeacon William Nares' tribute to the nearby Emma's Well, one of the sources of the New River.   Nares was Archdeacon of Stafford and a canon of St Paul's Cathedral where he knew Robert Mylne, who was Surveyor to the cathedral's Dean and Chapter and also Chief Engineer of the New River.   In this capacity, Mylne had landscaped Amwell Pool and the two islands in the late 1790s.   Mary, Robert Mylne's granddaughter, later recalled: "Under the willow is a stone on which are the following lines of Archdeacon Nares, left by him on the table of the round room of Amwell Cottage [now Well House] after spending three months there about the year 1818:*

> *Amwell, perpetual be thy stream,*
> *   Nor e'er thy springs be less*
> *Which thousands drink who never dream*
> *   Whence flows the boon they bless.*
> *Too often thus ungrateful man*
> *   Blind and unconscious lives,*
> *Enjoys kind 'Heaven's' indulgent plan,*
> *   Nor thinks of 'Him' who gives.*

Above: *Between old and new: Thorpe's Farm (now River Cottage) beside the New River, overlooked by the glebe barn and the church in a Batty and Jukes engraving that must date from some time after 1797 when Amwell Grove, visible in the distance on the right, was completed.*

Below: *A similar scene in about 1900, with St. John's church rising above the trees, with a solitary boy wrapped in apparent contemplation on the footbridge.*

Above: *River Cottage and the New River Bridge at Great Amwell, about 1908.*
Below: *The Amwell Marsh New River Pumping Station (here called 'Waterworks') in Amwell Lane about 1907.*

The Great Amwell War Memorial, which is situated below the New River, pictured in the 1930s. Glebe Cottages can be seen in the background.

     The New River — and not merely the Pool — is an integral part of the landscape of Great Amwell. Beginning at Chadwell Spring (which was once in Little Amwell but is now in Ware) and augmented by further springs along its course, the New River supplied London with water and enabled it in its day to grow into the most populous city in the world. Its impact in the Lea Valley has been no less dramatic. Supplemented in the early 18th century by water from the River Lea, its flow boosted by three local pumping stations from 1847 onwards, the New River has contributed to the lowering of the local water-table. This in turn drained the marshes, encouraged the development of the village of Stanstead Abbotts, made possible the railway of 1843, and more recently promoted the gravel-extraction industry.

This is what it used to be like.

Above: *'This is what it used to be like'. A scene of 1905 hardly recognisable today. The junction of the Hoddesdon Road (on the left) and the Hertford Road (now Folly Hill) is today a traffic roundabout. Its earlier name was Pye Corner. The road ahead is the historic parish boundary of St Margarets (left) and Great Amwell (right). At the left edge of the picture is Streatfield House, now the site of a traffic roundabout.*

Bottom: *A further scene of a road without motorcars — the Chaplin family with their dog out walking on Pepper Hill in 1892.*

A quiet scene on the London Road (Amwell Hill) looking north towards Ware in about 1905.

To the south of the Pool is Amwell Lane, developed from a post-enclosure footpath through the marshes to the gas works (long gone), the railway station, Pye Corner and St. Margarets parish. The road leading westward from the railway station has been known by successive names Station road, Hertford Hill, Folly Hill. It forms the parish boundary, but the Folly Estate of post-war housing was originally designated the St. Margarets Estate, though it is in fact within Great Amwell parish.

Above the Folly Estate and the former common fields of the parish is the old turnpike road (now the A1170). At its summit, Pepper Hill and Amwell Hill meet in the vicinity of the Waggon and Horses public house, the Firs and Pepper Hill House. From here, Amwell Hill descends past the much-altered ancient manor house of Amwellbury to Lowfield Bridge which leads into Lower Road (formerly Lowfield Lane), past Concrete Utilities and an area of housing where once stood the firm's social club and swimming-pool, then past Sheepcote Farm and back to Amwell Pool.

Two views of Great Amwell from the north-west, with the New River flowing beside the London Road. Above: An 18th century view, drawn by the artist J. Feary to illustrate John Scott's poem 'Amwell' published in 1782. The road was then part of the Cheshunt Turnpike which ran through Ware to Wadesmill. Traffic declined after the coming of the railway, but increased on a massive scale after the Second World War. Relief came with the opening of the A10 by-pass in 1976. Below: Workmen tend the banks of the New River not far from Ware in about 1907. Amwell village is on rising ground in the distance.

HOMES IN HERTFORDSHIRE

A.P.C. WRAY
Building Contractor
CHURCH ROAD HERTFORD

TELEPHONE : HERTFORD 446

ON THE AMWELL ESTATE

Great Amwell has had far less new housing in this century than Stanstead Abbotts, but in the 1930s A.P.C. Wray of Hertford announced development of the "Amwell Estate" (now St. Margarets Road). A £25 deposit secured a three-bedroom house costing £440 — with the balance to be paid at 12s.10d. a week over twenty years.

Above: *An aerial view of Hertford Heath in about 1960. In the foreground are the Roundings. The London Road runs across the photograph from right to left, turns north to join the Roman road known as Ermine Street (Elbow Lane) for a third of a mile and then turns left towards Hertford, leaving Ermine Street to continue north as Hogsdell Lane. To the right of this second junction can be seen the village of Little Amwell, from where Downfield Road (The Street) disappears into the distance off the top of the photograph. The building site just above the centre is today Postwood Green, completed in 1962.*

Below: *Two Edwardian ladies pass opposite the recently-erected South African War memorial at the entrance to Haileybury College in 1903. The bend in the road marks the point where the new causeway of 1635 (now the London Road) diverged from the medieval highway from Hoddesdon to Hertford, which still meanders through the Heath to the green at Little Amwell.*

Hertford Heath.

Haileybury College.

1835.

Sir Arthur Blomfield's dome of 1876 at Haileybury College dominates the skyline of Hertford Heath.

AROUND AND ABOUT HERTFORD HEATH

As one comes along the road from Hoddesdon, the first sight of Hertford Heath is the dramatic dome of Haileybury. The village proper, however, begins just past College Green at the East India College Arms public house.

The section of the London Road at this point was built over a causeway of 1635 through what used to be known as Amwell Heath. This section ends just past the Silver Fox (formerly the Crown) public house where the road veers right to join the Roman road Ermine Street (Elbow Lane) for about a third of a mile to the Camelot public house (formerly the Townshend Arms). Here Ermine Street was crossed by Beacon Hill leading from Hertford to Beacon Heath — the name for this part of the heath because it was the site of one of the nationwide system of beacons lit to warn of the approach of the Spanish Armada in 1588. Just past the Camelot, the main road branches left for Hertford, leaving Ermine Street to continue northwards as Hogsdell Lane.

Hertford Heath is criss-crossed by ancient boundaries. Ermine Street was for centuries a diocesan, hundredal, parish and manorial boundary: the legacy of this historic division is that the built-up part of Hertford Heath is entirely confined to the east of Ermine Street. Only in the early 1990s was Hertford Heath constituted a single parish.

College Arms Hotel, London Road, Hertford Heath.

Above: *The East India College Arms at Hertford Heath in the 1920s. The RAC sign is to attract motorists who have yet to appear.*
Below: *A pony and trap passing the (now vanished) Havelock Arms public house on the London Road at Hertford Heath in about 1905.*

Hertford Heath.

Above: *The London Road at Hertford Heath in 1911 had four public houses of which two remain, though the Crown Inn of this photograph has been renamed the Silver Fox.*
Below: *London Road Hertford Heath (part of Roman Ermine Street) looking north towards the Townshend Arms (now Camelot) sometime in the 1930s. The second pair of houses on the right was bombed on 25 July 1944 and was replaced by a pair of bungalows.*

LONDON ROAD, HERTFORD HEATH.

Above: *London Road, Hertford Heath, by the Townshend Arms some fifteen years before the War Memorial was erected.*
Below: *The First World War War Memorial at Hertford Heath sometime in the early 1920s. Its erection was due largely to the efforts of Florence Barclay and was in position before the end of 1920 when she and her husband, the Revd. Charles Barclay, left the parish.*

Vicarage Causeway, Hertford Heath, in the depths of the winter of 1932. In the background can be seen Pondside Cottages (now part of Mount Pleasant). On the left, with the spirelet, is the Mission Hall of 1882. The houses on the left-hand side of the photograph have gone.

Vicarage Causeway (formerly Beacon Hill) leads to the village green of Little Amwell which is flanked by the 18th century Goat public house and the 19th century Holy Trinity Church. The green lies on an ancient north-south highway running roughly parallel to Ermine Street — Downfield Road (still popularly known as The Street). This leads from the green northwards to the old manor house of Gamels Hall and Rush Green and it marks the spine of the ancient settlement of Little Amwell. Mount Pleasant with its Victorian terraces leads south from the green into the now-wooded heath in the direction of Haileybury.

Above: *Holy Trinity, Hertford Heath, in the winter of 1932. Behind the railings and hedge was the underground water supply tank, installed in 1908 by the Revd. Charles Barclay and supplied by an artesian well in the Vicarage garden.*
Below: *The Village Pump and Goat Inn at Hertford Heath about 1910. The alehouse was here in 1756, but part of the building is two centuries earlier. The pump of 1898 with its Biblical text was the inspiration of Florence Barclay, novelist and wife of the vicar Charles Barclay*

"THE GOAT" INN AND VILLAGE, HERTFORD HEATH.

Above: The village of Hertford Heath in the mid-1920s . On the left-hand side is the 'Goat' public house, in the centre are Goat Cottages (now demolished), to their right is The Street (now Downfield Road) with Amwell Place Farm in the far distance. The pond on the right-hand side was filled in and added to the village green in 1937.

Below: Of this photograph of about 1930, all that survive are The Goat Inn and the village pump — and no doubt many of the children!

The Goat Inn, Hertford Heath.

Hertford Heath.

Dear P. Mrs E. gave me this card for you, thinking you would remember passing this pool of water with the

Above: *Continuing on to the back, this card posted in September 1904 says "... thinking you would remember passing this pool of water with the geese in just before we turned down that narrow road."   The 'pool of water' was the pond at Hertford Heath; in the background are the houses of Mount Pleasant.   The pond was filled in during 1937 after prolonged complaints about its misuse.   Otherwise, little has changed in over 90 years.*

Below: *A photograph of the village pond at Hertford Heath about 1930 which both recalls the past and heralds the future.   On the left the cattle drink from the pond, as they had done for centuries; on the right, the new 'lamp of learning' advertising the proximity of the school was a warning to motorists, here conspicuous by their absence.*

The Pond, Hertford Heath.

Above: Ware Road, Hertford Heath, in the 1930s. It was renamed Downfield Road in 1949 after the residents voted by plebiscite for the change, but it is still popularly known in Hertford Heath as The Street. Most of the buildings shown here have gone, including The Two Brewers public house, the village shop and Jaggs' bakery (displaying the 'Hovis' sign in the distance on the right) and cars have replaced the cattle being driven to the pond.

Below: Mount Pleasant, Hertford Heath in about 1910 — with the village green in the distance. This view is today obscured by dense underwood, the result of the absence, since the end of the Second World War, of the grazing animals which fed on the young shoots of bushes and trees.

A drawing of the Hoddesdon Road at St. Margarets by Charles Whitley in 1882 when the sole visible development consisted of St. Margarets Church and the Crown Inn in the distance.

ST. MARGARETS: AROUND THE PARISH

Stanstead St. Margarets, or for convenience simply St. Margarets, is a long, narrow and small River Lea parish (408 acres) enclosed on three sides by Great Amwell.

The route begins at the Fisherman's Friend (once the George and Dragon) public house beside the River Lea, passes St. Margarets railway station (which is in fact in Great Amwell parish), and proceeds westwards along Station Road (which is also the parish boundary) to the small roundabout where once stood Streatfield House. South from here, the Hoddesdon Road passes the Crown public house (of 'House up a Tree' fame), St. Margarets church and manor house, Copping's nurseries, terraces of late Victorian houses and the Clock House, all that survives of the former Goldingtons manor house that once stood to the east of the road. The flyover of 1987 marks the effective southern limit of St. Margarets parish. Chardingleye Farm marks the effective western limit of St. Margarets, though the parish itself extends deep into the woodlands.

Opposite page, top: St. Margarets and Stanstead Abbotts from the air in the 1950s. The railway, River Lee Navigation and the Mill Stream run from top left to bottom right. At the left edge is part of the meandering Hoddesdon Rd with the nurseries, Clock House and St. Margarets church. The Roydon Road is at the top right. Connecting them is the Hertford Road (Folly Lane) and Stanstead Abbotts High Street.

Bottom: Another view of St. Margarets from the air. The four corners illustrate different phases of the history of the parish. Clockwise from top right: Clock House, marking the precinct of Goldingtons Manor House which burned down in the early 19th century; St. Margaretsbury of 1890, marking the end of a period when the squire was also the parson; the roundabout built on the site of Streatfield House; and St. Lawrence Avenue, then in the course of being built, which marks the onset of St. Margarets' most recent phase of development. In the centre, the ancient church with its bell-turret is hardly visible; above it is the late-medieval priest's house, altered in the 17th century and adapted in the 19th century by Joseph Pratt as a rectory and manor house to replace Goldington's.

Above: *The level-crossing at St. Margarets railway station looking west towards St. Margarets village in about 1905.   Lichfield House Terrace can be seen on the left of the picture.*
Below: *Lichfield House and Terrace, built in 1895, just by the level-crossing at St. Margarets, home and business centre of James Wells, cab proprietor.*

Lichfield House and Terrace.

Above: The Crown at St. Margarets in the Hoddesdon Road. The 'House up a Tree', for which this public house enjoyed a local fame, can be clearly seen.
Below: An idyllic view of the bridge over the New River at Hertford Hill (now Folly Hill) St. Margarets in 1905. There is no hint of the huge volume of traffic that this bridge was to bear later in the century.

Above: Ninety years after this photograph was taken, the Hoddesdon Road in St. Margarets has changed very little. The garden wall on the left was part of a higher wall that once encircled Goldingtons Manor House which burned down in the early 19th century.

Below: An early 20th century view of St. Margarets Manor House seen immediately to the left of the terrace of houses of 1889 that front the Hoddesdon Road. The former wooden tithe-barn on the left was used as a parish hall before being converted to a private dwelling. More recent buildings and mature foliage have long obscured this view.

Summertime at St. Margarets, engraved on glass by Arthur Swallow for St. Margaret's Church in 1987. The central panel shows the Rye Marsh pumping station of 1882 and the A414 Stanstead Abbotts flyover built in 1987. At the bottom is the Greenwich Meridian marker post erected in 1984 near the entrance to Amwell View School. Among the nettles and thistles in the lower right corner are two anglers — commemorating a pursuit for which the area has been famed since the time of Izaak Walton's Compleat Angler *of 1653.*

Above: St. Margarets Great Eastern Railway (GER) station about 1905. It was originally built to the south of the Hertford-Stanstead road in St. Margarets parish but was moved to its present position in Great Amwell in 1863 when the branch line to Buntingford was opened (it closed exactly a century later). In order not to confuse passengers, it retained its original name. In the right background stands the train for Buntingford. In the distance can be seen the St. Margarets Maltings (with spire) of 1866 and the sidings which were constructed to serve them.

Below: A train from London arriving in the early 1930s. St. Margarets kept the atmosphere of a country station until electrification in 1960. The Buntingford Line platform is on the left.

A train arriving at St. Margarets Station in July 1894. Above the train can be made out the cowls and spire of the St. Margarets Maltings.

ST. MARGARETS RAILWAY STATION

The railway is a common link between three of these four communities: the former Great Eastern Railway line runs through Great Amwell and St. Margarets and serves Stanstead Abbotts. The railway also originally ran through Little Amwell until 1894, when the northern rim of Little Amwell parish was transferred to Ware.

The railway station originally stood in the parish of St. Margarets but was moved 100 yards or so north of the Hertford-Stanstead Road to provide for a new common platform when the branch line to Buntingford was opened in 1863.

The railway rapidly replaced the barge as the principal means of conveyance of malt from Ware and also became the principal passenger highway of the Lea Valley. As these pictures make clear, however, it did not replace the barge for conveying malt from Stanstead Abbotts. Even as late as the 1890s, the local miller was using water transport not only for his flour but also for personal conveyance. By this time, however, boats on the River Lea were increasingly used for pleasure and less for business, a development that was associated with the rise of Rye House as a leisure centre.

The railway contributed materially to Stanstead Abbotts' brief fame as a mecca for day-trippers from London, and in due course generated commuter use. It also employed a considerable local workforce, from staff at St. Margarets station (20 in the late 19th century) to plate-layers and level-crossing keepers. A dramatic decline in 20th century use, symbolised by the closure of the Buntingford branch line under the Beeching cuts in 1963 led to a corresponding decline in railway employment. With the increasing 'gridlocking' of the motorways, however, the railway promises once more to become the quickest means of travel along the Lea Valley.

Above: *The mid-19th century St. Margarets stationmaster's house in the late 1960s just prior to its demolition. The house remained when the station was moved north of the road in 1863. Part of the old sloping platform is visible at the right-hand edge.   A nice horticultural touch was provided by the line of standard roses, planted by the stationmaster, Mr. Frederick Masters.*
Below: *The frontage of St. Margarets Station, L.N.E.R., in 1934.*

Above: *St. Margarets Station staff in 1922. The stationmaster, Mr. Frederick Masters, sits proudly upright in the centre of the group and to the right of him is the gate-porter, David Wheal, who was awarded the Edward Medal for bravery in 1912 when he pulled an old lady from the path of a down train. The full list of the passenger staff in 1922 was back row (left to right): Cyril Oliver, George Camp and Jack Fairly; middle row: F. Gabbatus, F.W. Head, Chris Burton, Ernie Vickers and W. Perry; front row (seated on chairs): Messrs Pavey and Hammond, Frederick Masters, David Wheal and W. Parker; seated on the ground: W. Roblett and B. Wick. The station then had a staff of 16 — 55 years later St. Margarets is manned on a part-time basis. Below: The level crossing in the 1890s, looking towards the river bridge and Stanstead Abbotts.*

Above: *Stanstead Abbotts from the Air in June 1968. The High Street runs diagonally across the photograph, meeting Cappell Lane and Roydon Road at the junction where the five gables of the Red Lion can be clearly seen. To the left of the junction is the large, solitary mill; to the left of the mill are the long buildings of French and Jupp's maltings. At the top of the photograph, boats are moored alongside the River Lea.*

Below: *The River Lea Bridge (formerly the Toll Bridge) seen from the north in the late 1920s. Stanstead Abbotts lies to the left (east) of the bridge and St. Margarets to the right. The prominent telegraph poles are a 'period' feature of the inter-war years.*

River Lea, Stanstead Abbotts.

Stanstead Abbotts Lock and House seen from the south. The Lee Navigation, though originally constructed in 1769 for transporting bulky freight such as malt, was also used for recreation, as in this postcard of 1905.

STANSTEAD ABBOTTS: AROUND THE VILLAGE

The village of Stanstead Abbotts is built over drained marshlands between the River Lea and the Mill River, itself a man-made stream (though today fed by the River Ash). The waterways brought trade and industry, but also recurrent floods. Central to the economic and social life of the village was the River Lea Bridge — in the distant past known as Thele Bridge, in more recent centuries as the Toll Bridge. Close to the bridge, there are few reminders today of the maltings, roasting factories and malt stores that once clustered about this point. Electrotest occupies the oldest surviving malting building in the village. Of the two riverside public houses whose wharves were the cradle of the local malting industry, only the Fisherman's Friend in St. Margarets survives, the Rose and Crown in Stanstead Abbotts having been demolished many years ago.

Photographs of the High Street reveal how often and how radically this street has changed its image in the last century or so. The dominant visual impression in the 1890s, when these photographs begin, is a compact one of working-class housing, small workshops (saddlers, butchers, bakers and blacksmiths), public houses and the cowls of maltings discreetly appearing above the rooflines. By the 1930s shops were increasingly the dominant visual feature of the High Street of this largely self-sufficient industrial village. With the sharp decline of the local malting industry, especially since 1954, the maltings themselves have mostly either been demolished or converted to other uses, and the shops have both declined in number and altered in character.

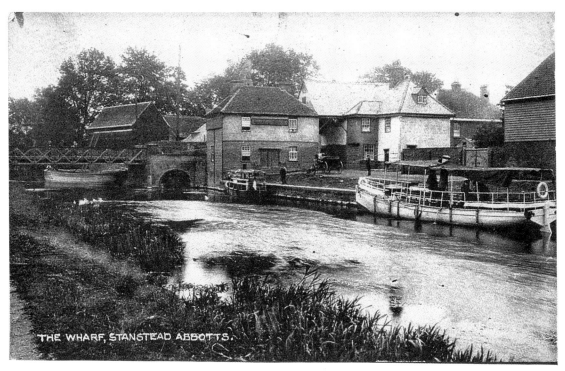

Above: *The former Toll Bridge and the Rose and Crown wharf in Stanstead Abbotts in 1905. In the background to the left and above the rooftops can be seen the buildings of Champion's vinegar malting. This wharf was one of the cradles of the local malting industry. In 1766, the members of the barge-owning Hankin family who ran the Rose and Crown built the maltings (just out of the picture on the right) on their wharf. The buildings survive, though malt is no longer made here, but the Rose and Crown was demolished in the 1960s.*

Below: *A complex of industrial and other buildings beside Stanstead Bridge about the turn of the century. Champion's vinegar maltings are to the left of the black weather-boarded building which displays the hoarding.*

Toll Bridge, Stanstead Abbotts.

Above: *The new bridge at Stanstead Abbotts in 1926.   After this time, the bridge carried more passenger traffic.*
Below: *A photograph of the early 1900s showing the main components that made the malting industry possible: maltings, houses, river and railway (behind the fence on the left).*

River Lea, Cottages.   This has been to China + Back

Above: *The full length of Stanstead Abbotts High Street looking east from the Lea Bridge in about 1908.*

Below: *Stanstead Abbotts High Street as it was in 1904. Charles Stevens, seen on the right, had gone from the Rose and Crown by December 1912 when this card was posted. This historic public house and nursery of the local malting industry has now been replaced by houses.*

High Street, Stanstead Abbotts

Above: *The 'pet revolution' and electric street lighting had already arrived at Stanstead Abbotts in this picture of the High Street looking east on a sunny afternoon in about 1932.*
Below: *By about 1950, Stanstead Abbotts High Street was begining to have a modern 'modern' feel. There were shops but they did not yet dominate the High Street.*

SAS.8.   HIGH STREET. STANSTEAD ABBOTS.   Copyright Frith Ltd.

Stanstead Abbotts. High Street looking East.

building at End is sort of "town hall." my house is to left there Vicarage to R.

Above: *A telegraph-boy and another boy wait outside Alfred Blackaby's Post Office in 1905. This postcard was the first to be published in the Blackaby Series on Stanstead Abbotts subjects. Boys often waited outside post offices hoping to pick up telegrams for delivery when the telegraph-boy was out on a call. Their services did not go unrewarded.*

Below: *Stanstead Abbotts High Street looking east when the motor-cycle and sidecar were becoming popular in about 1927. The garden of Stanstead Hall is on the left.*

Above: *Stanstead Abbotts High Street in about 1934 — not long after Mrs Maud Jones had opened her bakery shop and electric street lighting had been introduced.*
Below: *The High Street looking east on a sunny afternoon not long after the end of the Second World War. Cars are few, but they have already supplanted the bicycle.*

Above: *Stanstead Abbotts High Street from the Post Office to the Clock House in about 1920.*
Below: *The old world and the new — the High Street looking west in the 1930s. Electric street lighting has appeared, but the car has not yet pushed the horse and cart from the middle of the road.*

Above: *The earliest photograph of a small crowd scene in Stanstead Abbotts High Street at some time in the 1890s (Charles Newton whose name is on the Red Lion's sign had gone by 1899). Almost all the men, according to the custom of the age, wear headgear. The women have come to their doors either to learn what is going on, or to pose for the photographer, or both.*
Below: *Children in their 'Sunday best' in South Street, Stanstead Abbotts, in about 1905.*

Clock House, Stanstead Abbotts.

Above: *The Clock House and Red Lion at the junction of High Street and Chapel Lane sometime in the 1920s. Ominously for the future, the Red Lion advertises its 'free car park'.*
Below: *Stanstead Abbotts High Street seen from the eastern end in c.1905 at the end of afternoon school.   The Red Lion is on the right, the Pied Bull (advertising Hatfield Ales) is at the corner on the left.   The man on the right with the basket on his head was Bob Springham, fishmonger. The High Street, early in the 20th century, was still an amenity area, not yet sacrificed to traffic.*

Stanstead Abbotts Clock House seen from a point on the Mill Stream looking north. This photograph illustrates how radically this part of Stanstead Abbotts has changed in this century.

The east end of the High Street is the historic 'core' of the village of Stanstead Abbotts. Here the bridge across the Mill Stream originally abutted on to the medieval chapel which later housed the Baesh Grammar School and which gave its name to Cappell Lane (from Latin *cappella*, a chapel). Today it is known as the Clock House. The present layout of this area is the direct result of changing mill technology and mill fortunes. In 1893, the mill was converted from water to steam-power; in 1926, the mill closed altogether and the premises were occupied shortly afterwards by Burt's furniture and glass-fitting factory. Eight years later, the water being no longer industrially necessary, the Mill Stream was culverted and its bridge was incorporated into a comprehensive traffic roundabout.

South of the Clock House, Roydon Road was the original village street. It accommodates French and Jupp's Maltings (a lone survivor in this region) and the concentration of small workshops that occupy many of the former malting buildings. Farther south, the road forks: Netherfield Lane (once known as Elephant Lane) continues south in the direction of Rye Manor; Cats Hill continues past the Baesh Almshouses of 1635 and Netherfield House of 1830 to the ancient church of St. James and to Stanstead Bury, the manor house of the parish until 1824 when manor and estate were separated. It is likely that somewhere hereabouts is the site of the lost borough of 'Stanstede' mentioned in Domesday Book in 1087.

Left: *A rare photograph of the early 18th century weather-boarded mill at Stanstead Abbotts which burned down in 1865. The Clock House, which appears on the left, was still in use as a boys' school. A mill at 'Stanstede' is mentioned in Domesday Book in 1087, but it was not necessarily here. A mill on this site with its associated lock is first clearly recorded in 1666.*

Below: *After the fire of 1865, Stanstead Abbotts Mill was rebuilt in brick. Until the early 20th century, many houses fronting the Mill Stream had their own wharves, which gave access to the River Lea downstream — as in this postcard of Mill House wharf in c.1905. With successive improvements to the footbridge linking the High Street to the Roydon Road (its grille can be seen here reflected in the water below) these wharves above the Mill became increasingly isolated from their natural outlet and were eventually demolished.*

Stanstead Mill, Stanstead Abbotts, near Ware.

"Stanstead Abbotts." Mill Bridge.

Above: *The Mill Bridge at Stanstead Abbotts at the beginning of this century. The Clock House is just out of this picture on the right but St. Andrew's Church is clearly visible. The signpost to Chapel (now Cappell) Lane is to the left of the older boy standing on the bridge.*

Right: *The end of an era: the Mill Stream being culverted in 1934-35, eight years after the flour mill closed down. The footbridge was subsequently incorporated into a more comprehensive road layout.*

Two pictures of the Mill Stream from the Chaplin family album: Above: 'Arrived home, Stanstead Abbotts, 22.5.93' says the caption in the album.   This photograph shows the relationship of the Flour Mill (with lucam), Mill Stream, Mill House and Clock House in the distance.   The 'home' of the caption may have been Bachelor's Hall, which had a small landing-stage on the Mill Stream and which retains a boathouse to this day.

Below: Boating on the Mill Stream in 1893 for business.   The small weather-boarded building is the boathouse of Bachelor's Hall, which shared a wharf with the Pied Bull public house (visible in the background).

Above*: The Lyndsell family at a table in the garden of the Pied Bull in Stanstead Abbotts about 1890, with the sails of the long-vanished 18th century windmill visible above the roofs. Windmills in low-lying areas were often used for land-drainage rather than for corn-milling. Glenmire Terrace now stands near the site.*

Below: *Almost the same scene as that in the lower picture opposite — about 15 years later, but with the emphasis now on pleasure-boating although the Mill Stream continued to be used for transporting grain and malt. The St. Margarets address on this postcard was a means of informing would-be day trippers, pleasure-boaters and anglers which railway station they needed to use.*

The Pied Bull Landing Stage
Stanstead Abbotts   St. Margarets.

Above: *From the old wooden Fire Station to the former flour mill in Roydon Road, Stanstead Abbotts, in December 1979.*

Below: *Another view of Roydon Road, looking north. In the background can be seen the roof of the National School, partially obsured since 1912 by the Parish Hall.*

Stanstead Abbotts. Roydon Road looking North

The Schools in middle background Vicarage is just behind ... you

Three views of Roydon Road (also known as Vicarage Road) looking south. Ferndale on the right of the top picture of 1905 still exists as Abbotts House, but all the houses in the middle picture of the 1920s have been replaced. However, the Vicarage seen in the bottom picture of 1905 can still be seen today.

Above: *Cats Hill, Stanstead Abbotts, at the junction with Hunsdon Road in about 1935.*
Below: *The Stanstead Abbotts almshouses founded by Sir Edward Baesh in 1635 for six elderly women, each of whom was to receive 2d a week. This postcard dates from 1927.*

Above: *Hunsdon road, Stanstead Abbotts, in about 1912. The house on the right of the picture is still standing.*
Below: *Netherfield Lane, Stanstead Abbotts, probably before 1910.*

Cat's Hill, Stanstead Abbotts. 138273

Above: *A solitary car gingerly makes its way round and down Cats Hill (and on the wrong side of the road) in this postcard of 1928 — a very different view from the heavy cross-country traffic which the road carried in the 1960s and 1970s.*

Below: *Two views of the Stanstead Abbotts demonstration in favour of a by-pass in 1975.*

Above: *One of the many accidents that occurred at the bottom of Cats Hill before the heavy traffic of the A414 was diverted out of Stanstead Abbotts along the by-pass.*
Below: *How are the mighty fallen! The pollarded oak at the junction of the Roydon and Eastwick roads in all its glory in 1905... And (right) in January 1963, when a young oak had regenerated — or been planted — inside the trunk of the old.*

The junction of Cappell Lane, High Street and Roydon Road, Stanstead Abbotts, in 1936. The Prince of Wales public house and the upper part of the Countess of Huntingdon's chapel can be seen in the background. In the right foreground is the Clock House. This photograph shows how the culverting of the Mill Stream (beneath the Austin van) and more recent roadworks had isolated the Clock House from its historical setting.

North of the Clock House is Cappell Lane, named after the medieval field chapel (Latin *capella*) which stood on the site of the Clock House. Cappell Lane has also been known as Chapel Lane and Park Lane. On the right of the lane stood the chapel of the Countess of Huntingdon's Connexion built in 1874, now demolished to make way for a house. A short distance farther on is St. Andrew's Church of 1882 and the entrance to Easneye House, built for Thomas Fowell Buxton in 1869 to give the parish a new manorial centre. The projected manor of Easneye was stillborn, but Cappell Lane retains, especially in its up-market labourers' cottages, some of the characteristics of a Victorian 'closed' village.

Stanstead Abbotts. Chapel Lane.

Above: *Chapel Lane, Stanstead Abbotts, looking today very much as it appeared in 1907 when this photograph was taken. The principal changes have been the recent demolition of the Countess of Huntingdon Chapel (the bell-turret of which appears above the houses on the right), the closure of the Prince of Wales beer-house on the right, and the reversion to the older name of Cappell Lane.*

Below: *Park Road, an alternative name for Chapel Lane, Stanstead Abbotts, in the early 20th century when the 'villas' were still quite new. The parish council decided in 1931 to revive the much older name of Cappell Lane.*

Above: *Cappell Lane just south of Warrax House (of 1884) and Warrax Cottages in the early 20th century.*
Below: *The Retreat in Cappell Lane, Stanstead Abbotts, about 1910.*

St. John's Church, Great Amwell, from the south-east in 1902.

CHURCHES AND CHAPELS

Between them these four villages have five Anglican churches, three of them ancient and the other two 19th-century buildings of the Gothic Revival. There used also to be two early 19th-century chapels of the Countess of Huntingdon's Connexion — one in Stanstead Abbotts, the other in Hertford Heath — but now both have gone.

Great Amwell has the venerable Parish Church of St. John the Baptist. It is a church of considerable charm, presence and beauty.

Hertford Heath has no ancient church. It now has only one church, Holy Trinity, built in 1863 as the parish church of Little Amwell. Florence Barclay, wife of the second vicar of Holy Trinity, was in her day a well-known romantic novelist.

St. Margarets has what at first sight seems an unspectacular church. On closer acquaintance, however, this is seen to be a most engaging gem of an ancient church which has a curious and convoluted story, made the more fascinating by strange gaps in its documented history and unexplained oddities in its fabric.

Stanstead Abbotts has two Anglican churches. The ancient church of St. James on the hill by Stanstead Bury was the original parish church until 1882, and has preserved an authentic 18th century interior. Since 1882 the parish church has been St. Andrew's in Cappell Lane, designed by the famous Victorian architect Alfred Waterhouse for Thomas Buxton of Easneye.

Above: *The creeper-clad Church of St. John the Baptist, Amwell. The card was published before 1908 but not posted until 1911.*

Below: *A pre-1836 drawing of the old south vestry at St. John's church, Great Amwell. The Revd. William Harvey later noted "The vestry was first built on the south side of the chancel, 1810 ... It was found to be too hot in summer, and in 1836 was removed to the north side."   The small building on the right is the mausoleum of the Mylne family.*

Two views of the tower and entrance to Great Amwell church: the one on the left is an engraving which was published with John Scott's poem Amwell *in 1776 — "the gentle Bard ... by Fame forgotten" was the Elizabethan poet William Warner who is buried in the church. The photograph right, taken on Boxing Day 1892, shows a typical wrought-iron lamp of the period.*

Right: *The bells of St. John's Church being repaired as a memorial to King George VI. The two larger ones, lying on the ground to the right, were renamed 'George' and 'Elizabeth' before being re-erected in the tower in time to peal in the New Year of 1953.*

Above: *The nave of Great Amwell church looking east. The romanesque chancel arch is original. The Jacobean pupil in the left (north-east) corner was brought here by Robert Mylne from the archbishop's palace at Croydon at the turn of the 19th century. The large stained-glass window at the right-hand edge was erected by subscription of the children of the parish at Easter 1857.*

Left: *The Vicar of Great Amwell, the Revd. Edward Walker, celebrating the fiftieth anniversary of his ordination as a priest in 1992 in the presence of the Archbishop of Canterbury, the Most Revd. Robert (now Lord) Runcie.*

The nave of St. John's Church, Great Amwell, looking west in a photograph of the 1920s. The present ringing-gallery of the church was constructed as a memorial to King George VI in 1953.

Hertford Heath. Church.

Above: *Holy Trinity Church, Hertford Heath, in about 1910. It was built in 1863 in the then fashionable Early English neo-Gothic style as the parish church of the Liberty of Little Amwell by the Rev David Barclay Bevan of Amwellbury, who became its first vicar, on land donated by Viscount Townshend, lord of the manor of Little Amwell. It was expected that the local community would grow after the re-opening of Haileybury College in 1862. There was then no further need of the chapel-of-ease which had been housed in the National School building of 1837.*
Below: *An unusual view of Hertford Heath church from the south-east, about 1905.*

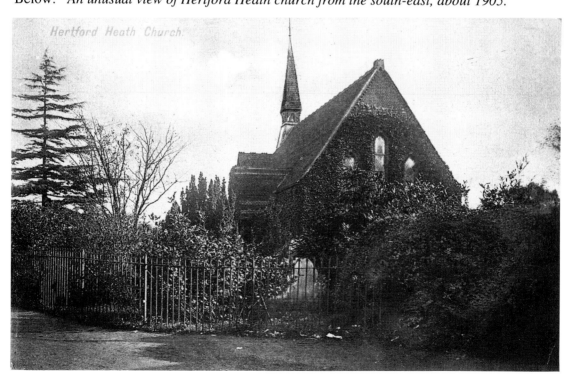

Hertford Heath Church.

Living Annual value £6
St. Margaret's Church near Ware.

Above: *St. Margaret's, until 1903 a 'donative' church (a private possession) as discreetly screened from view in about 1907 as it is today. The patron, the lord of the Manor of Goldingtons, was required to pay the incumbent (vicar) £6 a year. Until 1889, when the Revd. Charles Pratt died at the age of 96, the patron and the incumbent were one and the same person.*
Below: *St. Margarets church from the north-east in 1903. Since that time, some of the rendering seen here on the north wall has been removed to reveal a blocked arcade of the 14th century collegiate church.*

St. James' Church, Stanstead Abbotts

Above: *St. James's Church, Stanstead Abbotts, was no longer regularly used after 1882 when St. Andrew's was consecrated and became the parish church. In this picture of the 1920s, Stanstead Bury can be seen in the background behind the church.*

Below: *St. James's 'old' church, Stanstead Abbotts, from the north-west. The church had belonged to the canons of Merton Priory in Surrey from the 12th century until the priory was dissolved in 1536, and was acquired by Sir Edward Baesh, together with the manor, in the 1550s. It was he who in 1577 built the brick chapel shown here on the left (Copyright: National Monuments Record).*

St. James, Stansread Abborts.   114253.

Above: *Stanstead Abbotts' own time-warp: the interior of St. James's church showing the 18th century box-pews and 'three-decker' pulpit. Regular services had been discontinued for just over 20 years when this photograph was taken in 1904.*

Below: *Inside the Baesh chapel of 1577 beneath its plastered waggon roof. Sir Edward Baesh died aged 80 in 1587 and is commemorated in the monument at the far end of the north wall where he is described as 'Generall Surveyor of the victuals for the navy royal and the marine affayres within the realms of England and Ireland'. In the east window (ahead) are the arms of Queen Elizabeth I who held court at Stanstead Bury in 1571 and 1576 (Copyright: National Monuments Record).*

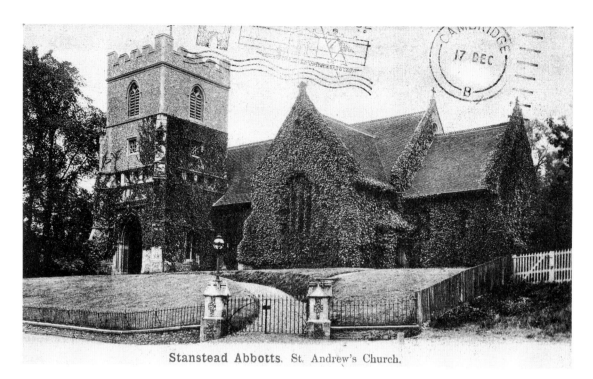

Stanstead Abbotts. St. Andrew's Church.

Above: *The 'new' church of St. Andrew's which replaced St. James's as the parish church of Stanstead Abbotts in 1881. Though only 30 years old in this postcard of 1911, it already looks ancient and venerable.*

Below: *The nave and chancel of St. Andrew's Church, Stanstead Abbotts, built by Alfred Waterhouse in the perpendicular style for Thomas Fowell Buxton of Easneye in 1881. This photograph of 1905 clearly shows that meticulous attention to medieval detail (including the hammer-beam roof of the nave) for which Waterhouse was celebrated in his day.*

St. Andrews Church Stanstead Abbotts near Ware.

The Countess of Huntingdon's chapel in Cappell Lane, Stanstead Abbotts, had originally opened
*in 1808, though the building shown in this postcard of 1907 dated from 1874. The chapel joined
the Hertfordshire Congregational Union in 1905 and appointed the Revd. F. Higgins as minister.
After his retirement in 1933, the chapel declined in membership and closed in 1984. In 1988 the
building was demolished and replaced by a house.*

      The Countess of Huntingdon's Connexion took its name from the 18th-century countess,
Selina Hastings, who left the Methodists to found a more Congregational form of worship. They
had two chapels in the four villages — one at Stanstead Abbotts, the other at Hertford Heath, and
both were originally served by students from Cheshunt College. The chapel in London Road,
Hertford Heath was founded in 1829 by Francis Johnson, a Professor of Sanskrit at the East India
College, out of the profits of a Persian and Arabic dictionary dictionary that he compiled. It closed
in September 1991 and by September 1996 had been completely demolished. The chapel at
Stanstead Abbotts was founded in 1808, but surviving photographs are of the rebuilt chapel of
1874. It closed in 1984 and was demolished four years later. In its day, its Sunday School 'treats'
were legendary. The last minister and the congregation of the chapel are shown on p. 177.

INNS AND PUBLIC HOUSES

In the history of villages like the four in this book, public houses were an important social institution. Like churches, they came in differing sizes, in ranks of esteem and in very uneven patterns of distribution. They were as common in Stanstead Abbotts as they were rare in Great Amwell. Tiny St. Margarets had two pubs but Hertford Heath, a poorer but populous community, had seven.

Vying for the first place in public esteem in Stanstead Abbotts were the Red Lion and Pied Bull, each with its own wharf beside the Mill Stream, a feature they shared with the now defunct Rose and Crown beside the River Lea Bridge. These wharves served the needs of commerce and, as these photographs show, were developing into leisure and social centres by the early 20th century.

Other public houses also sought to enhance their status through the lustre of a name with royal associations. The Rose and Crown of St. Margarets shortened its name to the Crown in the early 19th century partly to avoid confusion with its namesake in Stanstead Abbotts, while the 19th-century Crown at Hertford Heath has only recently abandoned its royal aura in favour of the Silver Fox.

The King's Arms at Rye House was perhaps the most ironic of all the local pub names in view of the association of Rye House with the alleged conspiracy of 1683 against the lives of King Charles II and his brother, the Duke of York. But for vaulting ambition from humble village alehouse to a hostelry fit for gentlemen, the palm must go to the Quart Pot of Great Amwell which re-invented itself as the King's Arms after 1834 and as the George The Fourth in the 1890s, when it also acquired its present facade. On the other hand, the fate of the Queen's Head and the Prince of Wales in Stanstead Abbotts are a reminder that prestigious names alone were no substitute for a solid bedrock of business: like the Five Horse Shoes they are long gone.

Since none of these public houses was on a main road, the presumption must be that they catered mostly for a local trade. The two different types of patron envisaged by publicans — the local villager and the passing traveller — are vividly illustrated at Hertford Heath where the London-Hertford road passes near, but not through, the ancient village.

The Goat had been the village alehouse since the mid-18th century. The two other vanished 'locals' in Downfield Road — the Two Brewers and the Horse and Dray — as the photographs on the following pages show, never rose above the rank of small beer houses. On the other hand, the four public houses that fronted the London Road (to which may be added a fifth, the Galley Hall in Hailey Lane) were designed to tap a passing trade generated by Haileybury College. Thus the Jolly Pindar of 1808 was renamed the East India College Arms, while the Townshend Arms was designed to capture the same passing trade for the benefit of Little Amwell, its name (until it was renamed Camelot in 1996) being in honour of Marquess Townshend of Balls Park, the lord of the manor of Little Amwell.

Yet sites alone are no guarantee of prosperity. While the Waggon and Horses on the main London Road at Great Amwell has survived, the Havelock Arms on the London Road at Hertford Heath has vanished, and the owners of the Crown and the Townshend Arms at Hertford Heath have both deemed it wise to change their long-familiar names.

Above: *John, Elizabeth and William Hunter pose with family and customers in the forecourt of their public house, the George The Fourth, shortly before it was rebuilt in the 1890s*
Below: *A horse, with its farm-cart attached, patiently waits outside the appropriately-named Waggon and Horses public house at Great Amwell in c.1893*

Above: *'Lower Sally's', the Haileybury boys' nickname for the Galley Hall in Hailey Lane where saveloys & hot potatoes were sold through a window by Sally, a former servant at the East India College. It is now a public house.*
Below: *The East India College Arms and Hotel at Hertford Heath in the 1920s. An earlier name, The Jolly Pindar, is first recorded in 1808.*

THE COLLEGE ARMS HOTEL, HERTFORD HEATH.

The Goat Inn. Hertford Heath. C.D.Soar.1930.

Above: *The Goat inn at Hertford Heath as it may have been in 1630, drawn by C.D. Soar in 1930. Part of the building seen here was in existence in 1630, and it may even have been an alehouse at that time.*
Below: *The Crown Inn at St. Margarets in 1905 with the feature known locally as 'the House up a Tree'*

The Crown Inn. The House up a Tree. C. Turner, Proprietor   1905

Above: *The former Rose and Crown public house at Stanstead Abbotts, probably at some time in the 1960s shortly before its demolition.*
Below: *The Pied Bull was still at the business and social heart of Stanstead Abbotts in the 1930s.*

Pied Bull Hotel, Stanstead Abbotts.

"Red Lion" Hotel, St. Margarets, Ware, Herts.

Above: *The Red Lion, formerly an inn, now a 'hotel' in this Edwardian postcard. The St. Margarets address for a Stanstead Abbotts hotel is probably explained by the need to make its whereabouts known to railway travellers.*
Below: *The still-largely unchanged Red Lion thirty or so years later.*

Above: *The Red Lion at Stanstead Abbotts in 1908 when Charles Harper was the proprietor, as this postcard informs the recipient no less than three times.*
Below: *The Five Horse Shoes, Stanstead Abbotts, about 1903, shortly after Charles Moberly and his wife took over the public house. The house, re-built in 1893, as the terracotta tile informs us, is now the site of Horse Shoe Close.*

Amwellbury, the home of Colonel Brown, lord of the manor, as depicted by John Hassell in 1817. Only the lower wing on the right survives.

MANOR HOUSES

Of the manor houses in these four villages, Stanstead Bury is the only one of stately-home rank. Since the dissolution in 1539 of Waltham Abbey, whose monks owned the manor, Stanstead Bury has been principally associated with the Baesh, Feilde and Trower families. It was the manor house of Stanstead Abbotts until 1824 when the manor was separated from the estate by William Feilde. Amazingly, it has survived in a 20th century of escalating costs and unsympathetic legislation as both a family home and a living museum of architectural styles and tastes.

Easneye had the style and pretensions of a manor house, but was never one in fact. Completed by the architect Alfred Waterhouse for Thomas Fowell Buxton in 1869, Easneye House was celebrated in its day for its generous use of terracotta. Today, Easneye is the home of the All Nations Christian College.

Amwellbury has not been so fortunate in its owners as Stanstead Bury. The large 17th century house, to judge by the Heath Tax returns, was completely rebuilt in the 18th century but was never a house to match Stanstead Bury in architectural grandeur. More alterations in the 19th century changed its appearance, and massive demolition in the 1950s of 'uneconomic' wings reduced Amwellbury to the size and status of a country house. Of the 17th century house, only the dovecot survives.

Above: *Edwardian high summer at Amwellbury in about 1910.   Since the 1950s, much of the house situated in Walnut Tree Walk has been demolished.   During and just after the Second World War, the house was a private school, known as Pinewood and run by Edna Kenyatta, the English wife of the Kenyan independence leader.*
Below: *Amwellbury in 1954 — much as it looks today.*

Above: *The Billiards Room of Amwellbury in 1891 when it was the home of Ernest Feling, a 42-year old stockbroker. The table was lit from above by six ornate oil lamps supplemented by an oil standard lamp at the side (Copyright: National Monuments Record).*

Below: *The drawing-room at Amwellbury in 1891. The decor and furnishings are a good example of a typical upper middle-class Victorian interior (Copyright: National Monuments Record).*

Above: *Part of Gamels Hall, Hertford Heath, in about 1970. The house is next to Rush Green, the site of the medieval manor of Rushen or Little Amwellbury.*
Below: *The Keep at Gamels Hall, Rush Green, Hertford Heath in 1970.*

Part of Gamels Hall, Hertford Heath, in 1957. (Copyright: National Monuments Record).

The name of Gamels Hall in Hertford Heath derives from 'Gamaliel', a late medieval occupier.   The hall is the 17th-century successor to the manor house of Rushen *alias* Little Amwellbury, founded by the canons of Waltham in the 12th century at Rush Green, the site of which was in the immediate vicinity. The construction of a major roundabout in the 1980s next to the A10 by-pass destroyed much archaeological evidence, but fortunately did not destroy Gamels Hall.

St. Margarets manor house from the north-west in 1972. Part of the house, which contains a Pre-Reformation religious mural, is of late medieval origin, and may have been a priest's house. It became the manor house after the destruction in the early 19th century of Goldingtons Manor House on the opposite side of Hoddesdon Road (Copyright: National Monuments Record).

St. Margarets Manor House is a gem. It was not a manor house originally, nor is it one today. The parish of St. Margarets was historically associated with two ancient manors, Hailey and Goldingtons, and a rare 16th century map places Goldingtons on the site later occupied by Hailey Hall. Whatever the explanation, by the early 18th century, Goldingtons manor house lay to the south of St. Margarets church and to the east of the Hoddesdon Road: of this house, only the Clock House (the former stables) survives.

After the destruction of Goldingtons manor house in the early 19th century, the former priests' house of St. Margaret's Church was remodelled as St. Margarets manor house. This development was facilitated by the fact that for much of the 19th century, the lords of the manor were also rectors of the church. With the death of the Revd. Charles Pratt in 1889, this link was broken, and his successor, the stockbroker Septimus Croft, built St. Margaretsbury to the west of the New River as yet another new manor house in 1890. Today (1997) St. Margarets Manor House has been divided into two, and St. Margaretsbury has been converted into apartments.

Above: *The drawing room of St. Margarets Manor House in 1972.   Since this photograph was taken, a fragment of a late medieval religous mural has been exposed in this room (Copyright: National Monuments Record).*

Below: *A fragment of a religious mural, showing angels blowing trumpets, recently exposed in St. Margarets Manor House.   It probably dates from before the Reformation.*

St. Margarets, Bury.

Two views of St. Margaretsbury: the photograph above of the front dates from about 1905; that below of the rear seen from the south-west (Copyright: National Monuments Record) dates from 1981. The house was built for the stockbroker Septimus Croft in a classical style immediately after he bought the property in 1889 . It incorporates part of the older rectory. Today it is divided into apartments.

THE REE.

Drawn on Stone from the Original Engravings by C.L.Tyler.

Above: *An engraving of Stanstead Bury published by Mullinger of Bishops Stortford in 1826, when Edmund Feilde was the owner. The engraving shows not merely the manor house, but also the old church of St. James and, in the top left corner, a representation of Rye House.*

Below: *The embattled gatehouse at Rye House, all that remains of the Manor of Rye which Sir Andrew Ogard was allowed by royal licence to 'impark and fortify' in 1443. The house achieved notoriety in the Rye House 'Plot' to murder Charles II and his brother, the Duke of York, on their way back from the Newmarket races in 1683. In the 18th century, the gatehouse was used as the Parish Workhouse of Stanstead Abbotts.*

Engraved by John Pye, from a Drawing by J.C.Smith.

For the Beauties of England and Wales, E.W.Bdr.

THE RYE HOUSE,

Above: *Stanstead Bury in all its assymetrical glory, as drawn in 1902 by the Hitchin artist, Frederick Landseer Griggs for the book* Highways and Byways in Hertfordshire.
Below: *The stair hall and late 17th-century staircase at Stanstead Bury in about 1929.*

Two of the fine staircases at Stanstead Bury.

Right: *The stair hall and main staircase with carved fluted balusters of about 1690.*

Below: *A newel staircase connecting two floors of the 16th-century wing*

(Both copyright: National Monuments Record).

Above: *Easneye, Stanstead Abbotts, from the air at some time in the 1930s.*
Below: *The front elevation of Easneye , built by Alfred Waterhouse for Thomas Fowell Buxton in 1869 and now the All Nations Christian College.*

Great Amwell House, shown in this photograph of 1925, was originally known as Ware Hill House, having been built for Major John Ware, a wounded veteran of the Napoleonic Wars.He and his wife, Mary,who was a Greek and Hebrew scholar as well as a poet, attended Amwell church each Sunday in the company of three dogs. The house was later considerably altered and became the home of Sir Stevenson Blackwood, Secretary to the Post Office who, it was widely believed, used his influence to secure a second daily postal delivery in the village (Copyright: National Monuments Record).

COUNTRY HOUSES

Country houses are major social institutions in their own right and make a major contribution to the landscape. Those in Stanstead Abbotts and Great Amwell have contrasting origins. In Stanstead Abbotts they developed from farmsteads or village houses over a period of time, and are dispersed throughout the parish; in Great Amwell they were mostly purpose-built and are concentrated in the village centre.

There were country houses in the other two parishes — there is a photograph of Streatfield House in St. Margarets (see p.18) but none for Heathfield in Hertford Heath.

In Great Amwell, the earliest surviving country house is probably the late 18th-century or early 19th-century Ware Hill House (now known as Great Amwell House). It was built for Major John Ware, a wounded veteran of the French wars who died in 1836.

Most of the country houses in the village are associated with the architect and engineer Robert Mylne and his family, who collectively conferred on Great Amwell the image with which it has been identified ever since.

Above: *Amwell Grove in the 1830s. The Grove was the first house that Robert Mylne built for himself in Great Amwell in 1795-97. Its distinctive feature was a chimney stack at each corner.*
Below: *The much-altered Amwell Grove in 1953.*

Above: *The front rooms of Robert Mylne's Amwell Grove as they were in March 1972 (Copyright: National Monuments Record).*
Below: *A drawing made in the 1830s of The Mount as Robert Mylne built it at the turn of the 19th century. The house was destroyed by fire in the early 20th century and rebuilt to a different design.*

Robert Mylne perceived the aesthetic potential of landscaping the New River below the church, a process which began in the 1790s with the creation of Amwell Pool and its two islands. The process continued to the north-west with Amwell Grove, his own highly idiosyncratic summer residence, completed in 1797, and this was complemented by The Mount which overlooked the Pool from the south-west.   Only long after Robert Mylne's death in 1811 was the beauty of his Mylne's vision fully realised as the maturing trees lent grandeur to his concept of the Pool dominated by the ancient church. It was left to his son, William Chadwell Mylne, to complete the composition by shaping a fisherman's cottage into Amwell Cottage (now Well House) and Thorpe's Farm into River Cottage.

Above: *Well House, formerly Amwell Cottage, where in 1818 Archdeacon Nares wrote the poem 'Amwell, perpetual be thy stream'. Robert Mylne in 1797 bought the land — including part of Amwell Marsh and Emma's Well — from Anne Lake, lady of the manor, and added the house to a former fisherman's cottage. The new front was added about 1850.*
Below: *Mylnefield, Great Amwell, in about 1900. The oldest part of the house, which dates from the early 19th century, may once have been Robert Mylne's farmhouse.*

Above: *River Cottage in about 1905. Originally a 17th century building and known successively as Thorpe's Farm and the Lintz in the 18th and 19th centuries, it was remodelled as a country house by W.C.Mylne in 1811 and modernised by Robert William Mylne in 1891. For many years River Cottage has been the home of Mrs Elizabeth Sewell.*

Below: *The 'New' Vicarage of 1840 as it was a century later. This was in fact the second in a succession of houses that have been vicarages of Great Amwell. In 1864, the incoming vicar the Revd. Richard Parrott built Glebe House as yet another 'New Vicarage'. Today (1997) neither building is a vicarage, though the house in this photograph is still known as the 'Old Vicarage'.*

The second phase of house-building at Great Amwell was triggered by the enclosure of the common fields in 1837. This enabled William Chadwell Mylne to become a major landowner in the parish and sparked a rivalry between him and the vicar, the Revd. Mordaunt Barnard. The outcome was a spate of building on the ridge above the church in which the 'New' (now Old) Vicarage of 1840 was answered by Lea Court (now the Flint House) and Home Lodge.

The third phase of the country house in Great Amwell is one of improvement rather than new building and is associated with Robert William Mylne, the less controversial grandson of Robert Mylne. Filmer's Cottage which he remodelled in honour of Queen Victoria's Golden Jubilee in 1887 completed what was in effect a village of country houses.

Above: *The Flint House (earlier known as Lea Court) was built by William Chadwell Mylne in the years 1842-45 for the benefit of his wife, who found that Amwell Grove did not suit her asthmatic condition. This photograph with the two gardeners dates from some time in the 1890s.* Below: *Casts of the Elgin Marbles in the Flint House, Great Amwell. They were placed here in 1845 by William Chadwell Mylne when he completed the house in 1845 (Copyright: National Monuments Record).*

Left: Two mid-18th century relief figures of a naval officer with sextant and a seaman with rope in a ground floor room at the Flint House.   The architect and owner was William Chadwell Mylne, whose elder brother Robert had been a naval lieutenant who fought in the war with the First French Republic (Copyright: National Monuments Record).

Below: A 1916 sketch of the obelisk in the garden of the Flint House, commemorating the building of Blackfriars Bridge by Robert Mylne in the years 1760-69.   The obelisk originally stood beside that bridge but was brought here by his grandson, Robert William Mylne, in 1870 when Blackfriars Bridge was rebuilt and his own plans to replace his grandfather's bridge were passed over.

The Flint House in Great Amwell commemorates three generations of the Mylne family and their tastes in architecture and sculpture. It was built by William Chadwell Mylne in 1842-45 and its interior altered by his son Robert William Mylne in 1890. In the upper hall, William Chadwell installed plaster casts of the Elgin Marbles made by Lord Elgin before he sold the originals to the British Museum in 1816. In the garden, his son, Robert William Mylne, erected the obelisk from the old Blackfriars Bridge designed by his grandfather, Robert Mylne, in the previous century. Elsewhere in the garden are a statue said to be of the Duke of Wellington (now minus its head) and a piece of an observatory in Edinburgh. This last object was probably brought to the village by the Scottish-born Robert Mylne senior — as was the elaborately carved keystone of the Netherbow Port gateway which the owner of another house, Mylnefield, sent back to Edinburgh in 1972.

A Bit of Old Blackfriars Bridge
built AD 1760
Now in a garden at
AMWELL Herts.

RAMBLING SKETCHES

Left: *Home Lodge in 1950, when it was divided into two houses, Home Lodge and Walton Lodge. It began as a coach house and stables for the Revd. Mordaunt Barnard's vicarage of 1840 and was built on land adjoining William Mylne's new Lea Court, where Barnard housed his noisy pupils from the East India College (now Haileybury) — much to Mylne's annoyance. Mylne bought the property in 1845 and converted it into Home Lodge.*

Right: *This Turret stood nearly in the centre of the former common fields on high land between Great Amwell and Hoddesdon. It was erected about 1814 by James Hodson of Hoddesdon, a friend of the Mylne family who studied astronomy and fitted it up with telescopes and a revolving roof. After the common fields of Great Amwell were enclosed, William Chadwell Mylne bought the Turret, moved it to the grounds of his newly-built Home Lodge in 1845, called it the 'New Observatory' and put a thatched veranda all round. It today stands in the garden of Walton Lodge.*

Above: *The Revd. Richard Parrott, his wife Harriet, their daughter Jessie and visitors sitting informally by the veranda at Glebe House in Great Amwell sometime in the later 1870s. In 1881, Richard Parrott was no longer living here but at the Vicarage built in 1840.*

Right: *Lily Arnold outside her home at Mar Lodge (now Pepper Hill House) in the Spring of 1893. An earlier resident, Mrs Cautherley, gave her name to the lane that runs alongside the house down to the village.*

Stanstead Hall in the High Street, Stanstead Abbotts, seen from both the front (south) and the back (north). The house was built in 1752 for Michael Pepper, the miller of Stanstead Abbotts. The crenelated circular brick tower attached to the west wall housing a cast-iron spiral staircase was added in the early-19th century to give servants access to the basement and attics (Copyright: National Monuments Record).

Abbotts House (formerly Fernside), Stanstead Abbotts.   A much altered Tudor timber-framed house, it is the architectural centrepiece of what was formerly the village street, now called Roydon Road. It is today the home of Mrs Vicky Burt (Copyright: National Monuments Record).

Of the country houses in Stanstead Abbotts, the oldest are the Tudor Abbotts House (earlier known as Fernside) in the Roydon Road;   Newlands, a 16th century double house subsequently much altered;   and Bonningtons, a late-17th century house rebuilt in 1725 by Ralph Byde which later descended to Salisbury Baxendale.

Quite the grandest house in the High Street, however, is Stanstead Hall, built in 1752 by the local miller as a mark of his new-found social status.

Netherfield House is an early 19th century house, associated with Sir Felix Booth of North-West Passage fame, but more particularly with his nephew Sir Charles Booth, the gin distiller, for whom the present house was rebuilt in an italianate style in 1860. It was bequeathed in 1959 to the Salvation Army as an Eventide Home for men. The home closed in 1989 and the house has stood empty for some years until 1997, when it was converted into flats.

Above: *Netherfield House, Stanstead Abbotts, rebuilt about 1860 in an Italian style for Sir Charles Booth, head of the famous gin family. For forty years, from 1949 to 1989 it was the Eventide Home of the teetotal Salvation Army, an irony not lost on local wits. In 1997 the house was converted into private dwellings.*
Below: *Mill House, Stanstead Abbotts in the summer of 1894. It has now been demolished and replaced by houses.*

Above: *Newlands about the year 1905. It was then the home of Admiral Sir Henry Nicholson, who had retired in 1897 after serving as Commander-in-Chief at The Nore. He died in October 1914.*

Below: *Willowthorpe House, beside the River Lea at Stanstead Abbotts in 1905, about forty years after it was built. It is now a retirement home.*

Above: *Amwellbury Farm in the early 20th century. A house of exceptional interest showing the development of a manorial farmhouse over three centuries: from the 16th century brick hall on the left (which was built on the site of a medieval grange of Westminster Abbey), to the two timber-framed and gable-ended extensions of the 17th century in the centre, and the 18th century brick house with a half-hipped roof at the far right (Copyright: National Monuments Record).*
Below: *Amwellbury Lodge in the early 20th century. It was built in the early 19th century by Colonel Henry Brown, Lord of the Manor of Great Amwell, for his coachman (Copyright: National Monuments Record).*

The dovecot at Amwellbury Farm may have been seen by Celia Fiennes when she set out from Amwellbury on her tour of England in a side-saddle in the 1690s. The dovecot has in recent years been converted to a private dwelling (Copyright: National Monuments Record).

FARMS AND SMALLER HOUSES

Farms may have declined in number and may no longer be major local employers, but they remain of immense importance in the economy and their buildings still form a major feature in the local historical landscape.

Farms, with public houses, provide excellent examples of vernacular buildings — that is, buildings of a local style using local materials. In this woodland area, the typical vernacular material was wood, but timber-framed buildings are now comparatively rare. Some of the earliest photographs show not merely timber-framed houses, pubs and farms, but also timber-framed schools, maltings, the flour-mill at Stanstead Abbotts — and even the earliest St. Margarets railway station. The gradual replacement of wood by brick, a process which began at Stanstead Abbotts with the late medieval chapel (now the Clock House), reflects changes in the pattern of local transportation which made it more economical to use bricks brought from some distance rather than timber from local forests. It is the process of suburbanisation, symbolised by the substitution of brick for wood, that is the key to explaining the present appearance of these villages, caught as they are in a 'limbo' between country and town.

Above: *Glebe Cottages of 1865 with some of their their residents and their provider, the Revd. Richard Parrott with his daughter Jessie. The photograph was probably taken not long before 1885 when Jessie married the curate, the Revd. William Harvey, who in 1893 succeeded his father-in-law as vicar of Great Amwell. Glebe Cottages were demolished in the early 1970s.*
Below: *Vanished grandeur — Izzard's Farm, which stood across the lane to the north of the Quart Pot (the George The Fourth) in ruins at the beginning of the 20th century. There was great enmity between Farmer Izzard and Robert Mylne, who owned Amwell Grove.*

Above: *Limes Farm, formerly Hillside, in Great Amwell in 1954.*
Below: *Sheepcote Dairy Farm, earlier known as Amwell Farm, in Lower Road — a complex of 17th century timber-framed buildings. This photograph was taken in about 1950.*

Above: *Hailey Farmyard, Great Amwell, as it was in September 1894.*
Below: *Chardingleye or Charlye Farm, St. Margarets — photographed before the First World War, about 20 years after it was first built in 1884. Then sequested in rural solitude, it is today dominated by the A10 interchange with the A414, Stanstead bypass.*

Above: *Easneye Park Lodge about 1910. Until the bridge from the High Street into Cappell Lane was improved, it was easier for carriages to get to Easneye through Ware than through Stanstead Abbotts.*

Below: *The Poultry Farm at Easneye in c.1905. It was built in 1868 by Alfred Waterhouse, the architect of Easneye House, as a model farm for Thomas Fowell Buxton.*

THE TERRACE. HAILEYBURY COLLEGE.

The Terrace at Haileybury College in the early 20th century, showing Wilkin's Portland stone screen of 1806 and Blomfield's dome of 1876.

HAILEYBURY

The history of Haileybury is usually written in isolation from that of Hertford Heath. This is understandable, since Haileybury is a national and international institution. But it is also symbolic. Mrs Mollie Matthews, whose husband was a member of staff but who lived in the village, wrote in 1959: 'Haileyburians still tend to ignore Hailey the place, and its inhabitants trouble themselves very little, I fancy, about the School.' The different worlds they each symbolised is epitomised in a contemporary description of Haileybury as the 'college in a wilderness', which summed up the sense of desolation that Hertford Heath induced in the civilised mind of the early 19th century.

Founded in 1806 to train civil servants for the East India Company's Empire in India, its interests have always transcended those of Hertford Heath. With buildings in an international classical style designed in 1806 by William Wilkins (of Downing College and National Gallery fame) and grounds landscaped in 1809-10 by Humphrey Repton, pupil of 'Capability Brown', the college was part of the aristocratic rather than of the local world. Yet, of the many subsequent additions since it closed as a training college in 1858 and re-opened as a school in 1862, it is Arthur Blomfield's chapel and dome of 1876, described as 'one of the best-known architectural set-pieces in Hertfordshire' which have given Hertford Heath its defining skyline image.

The house that forms the original core of the college was once occupied by the Reverend Thomas Malthus the celebrated demographer and polymath whose 'parish' was the world rather than the Hertford Heath where he resided for more than 35 years. On the other hand, Francis Johnson, the celebrated orientalist and another international figure, founded the Countess of Huntingdon's chapel in the London Road and appears to have shamed the clergy into making spiritual provision for the neglected local community.

Two views of Haileybury from the air: Above: *A phograph of about 1930 before the Dining Hall was built.   The junction of Hailey Lane and the Hoddesdon Road is in the background:*
Below: *An aerial phograph showing William Wilkins' original symmetrical square campus of 1806 entered from the west through an Ionic five-part screen in Portland stone.   The campus is the second largest in the country.   This composition of the Greek Revival is a landmark in the history of English taste.   Set within the campus is Arthur Blomfield's chapel and dome of 1876 (Copyright: Hertfordshire Mercury).*

Drawn on Stone by W.L. Walton.

Hahnemühle & Walton Lithographer

HAILEY HALL. *House*

The Residence of the late REV.ᵈ T.R MALTHUS Profeſſor of Political Economy at the East India College, Herts

Above: *The original Hailey Bury, here incorrectly captioned 'Hailey Hall', in an engraving made after the death of Thomas Malthus in 1834. Before becoming Professor of Political Economy at the East India College, he had published in 1798 his Essay on Population which is probably the most influential demographic work ever written.*

Below: *Hailey House in c.1910. This double-pile plan house with parallel gable roofs seen in the nearside angle pre-dates the College by some 90 years. Mrs Mollie Matthews noted the anomaly that this house 'used to be Hailey Bury in Hailey, and now is Hailey in Haileybury'.*

Above: *'The College Ladies', Haileybury, June 1889.*
Below: *The 'new' organ of 1902 in Arthur Blomfield's chapel at Haileybury College. This photograph was taken in 1904.*

THE NEW ORGAN, HAILEYBURY COLLEGE.

Above: *Running to Chapel at Haileybury in the 1890s. The practice was forbidden after the Master was knocked down in the early 1900s.*
Below: *Haileybury boys and masters (one wearing a mortar-board) on penny-farthings and a velocipede in February 1886. The school rule was strict: 'Bicyclists may only ride with a master'.*

Above: *General Sir John French, on 25 July 1903, unveils the obelisk to commemorate Haileyburians who died in the South African War (Boer War) of 1899-1902.*
Below: *The Duke of York (later King George VI) taking the salute when he and the Duchess (now Queen Elizabeth the Queen Mother) opened the Memorial Hall at Haileybury College on 7 July 1932.   The headmaster, John Talbot, is just to the right of, and a step behind, the Duke.   The photograph was taken from the College day nursery by Lily Sibley (now Mrs Lily Bean) with a Brownie Box camera.*

The earliest National Schools at Great Amwell. The first (above) was founded in 1858. It was described by a contemporary as 'picturesque and rustic, yet somewhat unsubstantial'. It burned down in February 1874 and was rapidly rebuilt and re-opened in November the same year. The sketch below showing both the rebuilt school of 1874 and the original schoolmaster's house of 1859 was drawn shortly afterwards.

Grammar School at Stansted, Hertfordshire.

The Baesh Grammar School at Stanstead Abbotts, founded in 1635 — as drawn by Buckler in 1834. It was still managing on its original endowment of £20 a year, but had ceased to teach Latin grammar. This building is now the Clock House.

SCHOOLS

All the present schools in these parishes were church schools in origin. There were public elementary schools in Great Amwell, Hertford Heath and Stanstead Abbotts founded by the National Society representing the Church of England. There were also Sunday Schools attached to the churches, though all of them had ceased to offer formal instruction in reading and writing by the time these photographs begin.

At Great Amwell, the first National school was built in 1859 on glebe land next to the churchyard. When this burned down in 1874, it was rapidly replaced by a brick building on the same site. The survival of this school until the 1960s underlines the continuing importance of the Church in elementary education in Great Amwell.

At Stanstead Abbotts, the 17th-century Baesh Grammar School, existing on an endowment of £20 per annum, had ceased to offer any teaching of Latin by the 1860s and had developed into a school taking boys of the parish who applied for admission (together with some from St. Margarets for a small fee). The chief spur to making a wider educational provision to include girls and infants was a desire on the part of those who supported the notion of building Church schools to anticipate parliamentary legislation that would make it compulsory for local bodies to provide secular elementary education. The Baesh Grammar School closed in 1879 and its endowment was converted to a Baesh Scholarship at the refounded Ware Grammar School (for boys), later passing on to Hertford Grammar School (now Richard Hale). The Baesh coat of arms and motto: 'Bold in God' is still used today by Presdales School in Ware.

There were at least two other small schools which have not survived and which have left no memorial in the local landscape – the private Amwellbury school and the 'school house' at Pye Corner, on the border of Great Amwell and St. Margarets.

Above: *A school class at Great Amwell in 1924. Doris Stevens (now Mrs Doris Field), still well known in St. Margarets, is second on the left in the back row.*
Below: *William and Annie Chessill, headmaster and mistress of Hertford Heath National School, with 31 of their pupils in this school photograph of about 1902.*

Hertford Heath school and schoolhouse in 1912.

The link between elementary education and the Church of England is well illustrated at Hertford Heath. Before Forster's 1870 Education Act, which set up the 'Board Schools', all elementary schools were run by the National Society (Church of England) or the British and Foreign Schools Society (the Free Churches). Before the 1870 act, elementary education was neither compulsory nor free.

Hertford Heath school was built in stages. The earliest part, built by the National Society in 1837 with a grant from the Treasury, is the range partly hidden from view by the tree in the postcard above. This original building doubled as a chapel-of-ease for All Saints Church in Hertford on Sundays before Holy Trinity was built. The gabled structure on the left was added in 1851, the schoolmaster's house in 1861 and the school room at the right-hand edge of the picture in 1870. These additions were built to cope with the increased numbers and in an attempt to anticipate the implementation of Forster's Education Act.

The school was rebuilt on another site in the 1960s and these buildings converted into dwellings.

The correspondent who sent the postcard above in September 1913 wrote: "The country round here is simply beautiful."

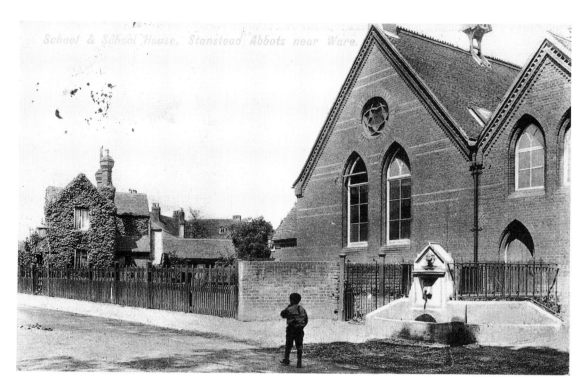

Above: St. Andrew's elementary school and school house at Stanstead Abbotts in 1904. The school was founded in 1869 — the year before Forster's Education Act was passed — with substantial financial support from Thomas Buxton. The first entry in the school log book on the 17 February 1869 runs: 'School opened by Mr Buxton and friends'. The first inspector's report of that year complained 'the children are extremely backward'. The grant was reduced by a fifth and the teaching staff was changed.

Below: A class of Stanstead Abbotts infants' school pose in their 'Sunday Best' for this photograph on 23 September 1909. The infants' mistress standing on the right was Mary Lovick (from Great Amwell, aged 25); Edith Clift (from Stanstead Abbotts, aged 24) was her assistant.

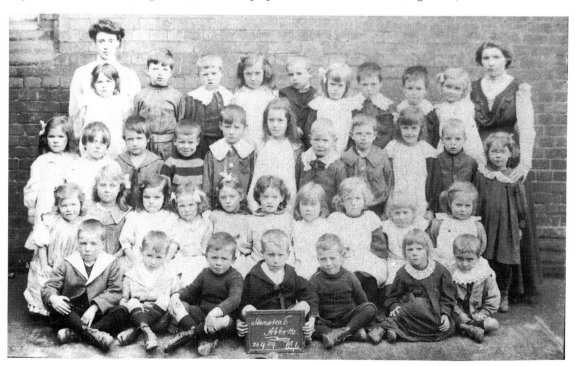

Above: *Stanstead Abbotts School, Standard IV in 1928. A rare photograph of a future husband and wife together in the same school photograph: Derek Kitteringham (later to be clerk to the Parish Council) is at the top left; his future wife Jean is second from right in the middle row.*
Below: *The girls of the senior class at Stanstead Abbotts School in 1946.*

Above: *The busy forecourt and wharf at French and Jupp's malting at Riverside Stanstead Abbotts early this century. The photograph brings out the close dependence of the malting industry on River Lea transportation.*

Below: *Part of the same range of buildings in 1965. The structure on the left (with the gambrel roof) dates from the 1770s when it was known as the Rose and Crown Malting and is another of the earliest surviving malting buildings in Stanstead Abbotts. The long brick building occupying most of the photograph was built in the 1870s in the days of the local malting industry's greatest prosperity. They closed as maltings in 1954 and have since been converted to other industrial uses (Copyright: National Monuments Record).*

French & Jupp's Roasting factory at Riverside, St. Margarets in 1962 when it was still making brown, black, chocolate-and-amber malt and roasted barley. The site has been turned into Riverside Green by the Lee Valley Regional Park.

INDUSTRY AND WORK

Of these four villages, only Stanstead Abbotts could be described as industrial. Though Great Amwell had a rope factory and concrete works and St. Margarets a paint factory, industry in those two places was peripheral: at Stanstead Abbotts, industry was integral.

Malting, a process which converts barley into malt for brewing into beer, grew up as a local industry serving the needs of the London brewers, especially those of Spitalfields. Hence the importance of good communications - water communications in the 18th and early 19th centuries, railway communications from 1843 until well into the 20th century. The Stanstead Abbotts malting industry grew from two originally separate bridgeheads: the Toll Bridge on the River Lea and the Mill Bridge less than half a mile to the east. Connecting them was Tollbridge Street, which has developed into the present High Street. The industry was nourished by the historic malting trade along the Ware River — the 18th century name for that stretch of the River Lea between Ware, the maltmaking centre, and London, the brewing centre.

Vital to this trade were the inns along the River Lea and their associated wharves, where, in the 18th century, the bulky grain and malt were stored ready for transshipment. The two inns by the Toll Bridge were the cradle of the local malting industry: the Rose and Crown (now demolished) in Stanstead Abbotts, and the George and Dragon (later the Railway Inn, today the Fisherman's Friend) in St. Margarets.

Left: *The Old Bakehouse of about 1700 — the oldest surviving part of French & Jupp's maltings and one of the oldest buildings in the village. French & Jupp's maltings still make malt, but parts of the complex have now been converted into successful small industrial units.*

Significantly, the earliest known maltsters who served more than a purely domestic or local trade had premises close to water transport. Among them were Richard Rumbold of Rye House (who was implicated in the alleged 'plot' of 1683 to assassinate Charles II and his brother), William Clarke (who built the earliest maltings on the Mill Stream in the early 1730s), and Thomas Hankin. Hankin was a barge-master and maltster with London connections who acquired the George and Dragon as early as 1720, bought out William Clarke's Mill Stream malting in 1734, and the next year became proprietor of the Rose and Crown with its wharf by the River Lea. It was this dominance of the local carrying trade that enabled Hankin to establish the malting industry in Stanstead Abbotts and St. Margarets.

Though water transport continued to be important, the Stanstead Abbotts malting industry was stimulated by four 19th century developments: the arrival of the railway in 1843; the construction in 1863 of a branch line to Buntingford designed to tap barley supplies from the north of the county; the simultaneous shifting of St. Margarets Station a few hundreds yards north to its present position in Great Amwell parish; and the almost-simultaneous building just outside the station of the large Abbey Maltings (then known as the St. Margarets Maltings) by Richard Hunt of Stanstead Hall.

Thus the malting industry spread westwards across the River Lea. Twenty years later in 1886 the St. Margarets Maltings were enlarged and in 1896 a roasting factory was built on the west bank of the Lea on the wharf of the Railway Inn — where the local malting industry had begun nearly 200 years earlier.

Right (top): *Floor turning of malt in 1954 at French and Jupp's in Stanstead Abbotts. An electric turner is being used in place of the traditional wooden shovel. In French and Jupp's modern malting, the germinating barley is turned constantly in huge drums rather than on a malting floor.*

Bottom: *Sacking malt at French and Jupp's for the Isle of Isla for whisky, 1960s*

The immediate effect of these changes was to double the workforce of the local malting industry, but from the early 20th century, the industry stagnated. New technology and structural changes in the malting industry nationally meant that there was excess capacity locally. As maltings closed and Stanstead Abbotts diversified its industrial pattern in response, so, ironically, it entered on its period of greatest prosperity.

The malting industry has left three legacies. First, some maltings have been pressed into other industrial uses. Secondly, as maltings have given way to houses, apartments and open spaces, so the resulting configuration of the village is still determined by the location of the former maltings. Thirdly, malt is still made in Stanstead Abbotts, whereas at Ware the malting industry has gone.

Left (top): *Abbey Maltings in Great Amwell, earlier known as the St. Margarets Maltings because of their proximity to the railway station, photographed here in 1972, shortly before a destructive fire. They were originally built in 1866 by Richard Hunt, the miller of Stanstead Abbotts and leased to Mary Hankin of the local malting family. The spire, which conceals a water-tower, added a touch of refinement to what are severely utilitarian buildings. They were enlarged in 1886 when the Stanstead Abbotts malting industry was at its peak, but shared in the slow national decline of the malting industry in the 20th century and closed in 1954. The whole industrial complex has recently been converted to apartments.*

Bottom: *Guy Horlock and Maurice Cracknell laying pipes for a new roasting factory at French & Jupp's at Stanstead Abbotts in 1962. Abbotts House, visible in the background, survives, but the intervening lake formed by gravel extraction has since been filled in.*

By the mid-20th century, the most important industrial employers were Burt's furniture and glass factory (now closed) housed in the former mill (which closed in 1926), Hankin's transport business in South Street (a successor to the 18th century firm), Wood's paint factory at St. Margarets, the new nurseries and the railway and the St. Margarets Gas Company; but the most rapidly-growing group of employees were those in the service industries associated with the rise in the number of shops, banks, cafes and other businesses, especially in Stanstead Abbotts High Street. Some of those changes are documented by photographs in this book.

Above: *The mill at Stanstead Abbotts was converted by the London firm of F.G. Burt to furniture manufacture and glass fitting after it closed as a flour mill in 1926. As the full car park suggests, this factory had become a principal employer in Stanstead Abbotts by 1966 when this photograph was taken. The 'glass factory', as it was popularly known, closed in 1991.*
Below: *A fully-laden waggon, with two drivers, stands in the grounds of the Mill in July 1894. The Mill House is in the background.*

Omissions from this book are themselves a social comment. Photographers had a natural predilection for rural rather than industrial scenes, for houses rather than factories and workshops, and hence their photographic records are apt to distort the relative importance of different aspects of local life. A photograph, for instance, of the washing of Haileybury College or of Christ's Hospital drying on the village green at Hertford Heath would have documented more graphically than words a distinctive type of employment there, but none, regrettably, appears to exist.

Left: *The Pumping Station at Amwell Marsh in the 1950s. The older building, which dates from 1869, survives; the building with the tall chimney, which was built by Frederick Hitch of Ware in 1883, was taken down in 1965 when electric pumps replaced the stream engines, and the building was severely reduced in size. The station still pumps more than three million gallons of water a day into the New River and has materially contributed to the lowering of the water-table in the Lea Valley.*

Below: *Workers at the 'Ropeworks' — G.H. Chaplin & Co., Gypsy Lane, Great Amwell, in 1911. The company was set up by George Chaplin in a cottage to the rear of The Firs in 1876 to make plaited packing as water-tight seals for the engineering and shipping industries. In two world wars, the company was a major supplier to the Royal Navy. Work at Great Amwell ceased in 1985, but Tim Chaplin still lives in Gypsy Lane and runs a similar company in Hoddesdon.*

Above: *The watercress beds at Rye House being tended by the Welch family in the 1930s.*
Below: *Concrete Utilities in the 1930s. The firm was established in Lower Road, Great Amwell, by the Australian architect Robert Marques in 1925.   From 1927, the firm made cable covers, artificial stone and concrete lamp columns.*

Above: *Great Amwell Post Office, on the east side of the London Road in June 1893. It subsequently moved to the opposite side of the road.   Mrs Maria Clarke, shown here holding a young child, was the sub-postmistress in the 1891 census.*
Below: *The Nook Cafe in Lower Road in Great Amwell about the end of the Second World War.*

Joseph Blackaby (centre) and six assistants pose outside an advertisement-festooned Post Office shop front in 1898. He was a baker as well as the village postmaster of Stanstead Abbotts.

SHOPS AND BUSINESSES

Because shops are characteristic of towns, it is surprising, not that these villages had few shops, but that the village of Stanstead Abbotts had as many as it did. The presence of industry was an important but not the only reason: there was some industry at Great Amwell but few shops.

The pattern of shop distribution largely corresponds with the observed pattern of 'open' and 'closed' communities. There were many shops at Stanstead Abbotts, and though there were never very many in Hertford Heath, at least there were more here than in either Great Amwell or St. Margarets. It is difficult to resist the local comment that these places lacked shops — as they lacked alehouses and nonconformist chapels — not because of a lack of demand, but because there was a tacit agreement that such development was undesirable.

Photographs illustrate the rise and recession of shops in Stanstead Abbotts High Street. Photographs of the floods of 1903, for instance, show the Oak public house and a temperance hotel, but little in the way of what would today be recognised as shops (see p.166). Later photographs show more houses being turned into shops with the process reaching a peak in the 1930s, where shops are the most characteristic type of High Street building. Since the 1960s in the High Street there has been a decline in both their number and variety.

Above: *The Snack Bar in the forecourt at St. Margarets Station in 1960. On the right is a train for Buntingford. The spire and cowls of the Abbey Maltings are in the background on the right.*
Below: *Brown's garage and petrol-filling station at St. Margarets where cars could be 'overhauled and painted'. All the buildings in this photograph of the 1930s were swept away thirty years later. The site is today the entrance to Lawrence Avenue.*

Above: *Frank Chappell's milk delivery cart outside the Havelock Arms public house at Hertford Heath in about 1945. The Havelock Arms was demolished some twenty years ago, but the Countess of Huntingdon's chapel, seen here on the far right, closed much more recently.*
Below: *Mrs Lou Stocker, photographed in 1955, with one of the fleet of mini-coaches which she and her husband operated from Stanstead Abbotts. Mrs Stocker still lives in St. Margarets.*

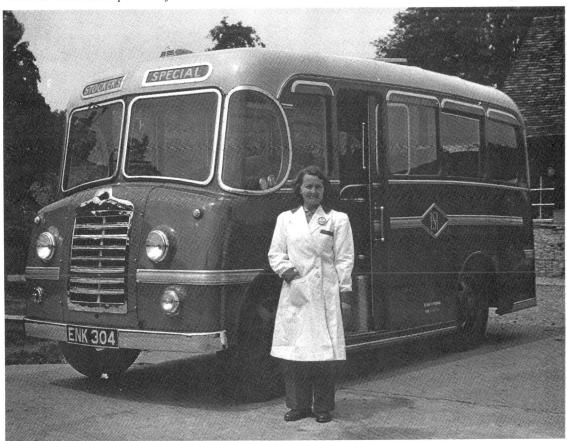

Above: *Blackaby's Post Office and agency for the Essex and Suffolk Fire and Accident Offices in the High Street, Stanstead Abbotts about 1900*
Below: *By the later 1920s, Blackaby's Post Office had become William Ray's general shop. More recently it was known as the Carpet Mill.*

High Street Stanstead Abbotts.

Above: *High Street on a fine summer's afternoon. Most of the buildings between Atkins'
pharmacy and the bridge have been replaced since this postcard was posted in September 1906.
The shop is still a pharmacy, however.*
Below: *Bert and Percy Anderson standing outside the hardware shop they had recently acquired
in the High Street in 1932. It then became known as the 'Stanstead Abbotts Stores (1932)'.*

Above: *John Bedwell stands by the horse and cart of his coal and coke business, at some time in the 1920s.*

Below: *The Vyses, father and son, and their display of traditional butchers' meat outside the family shop at 6 High Street, in this photograph of 1920.*

Above: *Mr and Mrs E.M. Brown at the door of their Post Office at 19 High Street Stanstead Abbotts, photographed in 1951.*
Below: *Elsie Turner and Mary Gould, shop assistants at the Enfield Highway Cooperative stores in 1938.   Look at those prices!*

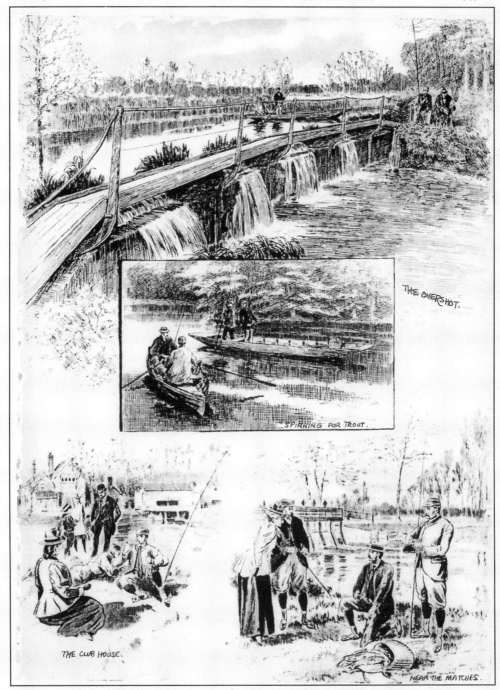

A FAMOUS FISHERY ON THE LEA---THE AMWELL MAGNA

The Amwell Magna Fishery at Stanstead Abbotts in 1895.   The caption of this drawing in the Illustrated Sporting and Dramatic News *reads: "Within a few miles of the smoke of the East End of London is one of the oldest fisheries on the Lea belonging to a club of 24 members who have carefully watched, stocked and preseved two miles of the old river still sacred to the memory of Izaak Walton and embracing that portion of the stream where the scene of the master instructing his pupil in the art of catching chub was sketched .... Having passed the Buntingford railway bridge ... we reach a long stretch of back water, and soon gladly welcome the club house depicted in the illustration."*

The Rye House Inn, with members of the Teale family in the forecourt, shortly before the sale of the premises to Christie's in 1904, when the 'inn' became a 'hotel'. The imposing cast iron window frames were brought by Henry Teale from a house in Cheshunt in 1870. In a building nearby Henry Teale installed the Great Bed of Ware, for which he paid 100 guineas.

RECREATION AND LEISURE

How did people of these village enjoy themselves out of working hours? Photographs generally lay more stress on organised than on spontaneous entertainment. Nevertheless, these photographs show a range of activities, though the evidence is, as elsewhere, patchy and possibly unrepresentative.

Among the historic outdoor pursuits of the Lea Valley is fishing, made famous by its association with Izaak Walton's *Compleat Angler* of 1653. The Amwell Magna Fishery was founded in 1831 and continues the tradition. It was to cater for anglers that the King's Arms at Rye House established its reputation in the early 19th century and the impressario William Henry Teale built up his Rye House entertainment 'empire' by initially exploiting its reputation as an angling mecca. Teale added all manner of attractions, including a banqueting hall, dance floor and boating. The East End bank holiday crowds who descended on Rye House by the train-load rapidly extended the sphere of their roisterings to St.Margarets and Stanstead Abbotts, turning the local pubs into a week-end extension of East London, much to the dismay of vestries and parish councils.

Another type of leisure-activity, under-represented here, was the annual fair. No photographs survive of the traditional Whit Monday fair at Stanstead Abbotts largely because it was stamped out as a result of 'disorderliness' in the 1880s. It is unclear whether the fair of 1921 at Hertford Heath was a survivor or a recent creation, the photograph published on p.147 being its sole documentation. The main distinction between earlier and later leisure pursuits was organisation. Whatever may have been the rough sports, punch-ups and pastimes of earlier times, the leisure activities portrayed in these photographs show a high degree of organisation, control and supervision, whether football, cricket or netball on the games field, or Women's Institute amateur dramatics in the parish hall.

Above: *Young 'milkmaids' dance round the maypole on the vicarage lawn (Glebe House, visible in the background) on May Day 1903.   This was a conscious attempt on the part of Mrs Jessie Harvey to revive the 'old revels' at Great Amwell.*
Below: *A Women's Institute party at Fernside (now Abbotts House) Stanstead Abbotts in 1925.*

Above: *The fair held in Kissing-Gate Field at Hertford Heath in 1921.*
Below: *'11 Feb 1895. An abnormally severe frost prevailing, a sheep was roasted whole on the ice near Stanstead bridge. The last occasion upon which such a thing was done in the neighbourhood of Ware was on 22 February 1855'* (Hertfordshire Almanac *1896*).

Above: *The Congregational Church annual Sunday School treat in 1898. The barge travelled from the River Lea bridge to the River Stort bridge and back. The 'treat' consisted of lemonade and currant bread, and games on a meadow beside the Stort. The next minister put a stop to this 'debauchery' in 1907.*

Below: *The captain and six crew members of the 'Mirabelle' at Riverside Wharf, Stanstead Abbotts, about 1920. Bill Kitt the captain, here seated on the extreme right, ran two pleasure steamers on the River Lea which plied between here and the River Thames.*

Above: *A Dick Whittington pantomime in the parish hall at Stanstead Abbotts in March 1934.*
Below: *Do-it-yourself home entertainment was still popular up to the end of the Second World War, as this Stanstead Abbotts Woman's Institute sketch of 1945 illustrates. But what were they performing that was giving the conductor (Daisy Darnell) such obvious delight?*

Above: *A fete in the garden of Mill House sometime in the early 1930s. In the foreground is the Mill Stream, shortly afterwards to be culverted.   This view has since totally changed and today houses occupy the site.*
Below: *The St. Margaretsbury Cricket Club's First XI in the early 1960s.   Familiar faces among the players include E.T. (Ernie) Pearce, headmaster of Stanstead Abbotts school, Benny Welch, Derek Kitteringham and Jack Lovick; the umpire seated far right is Albert Mead, who lived in St. Margarets Road, Great Amwell.*

Above: *The children's fancy dress parade at the 'Old World Fair and Fete' at St. Margaretsbury, 13 July 1946.   The weather did not match the sparkle of the occasion.*
Below: *Adult spectators at the 'Old World Fair and Fete' at St.Margaretsbury in July 1946.*

STANSTEAD ABBOTTS FOOTBALL CLUB,

SEASON 1920-21.

Winners East Herts League, Div. I.
Finalists Rolleston Charity Cup.

J. S. Robinson (Photo)   185-7 High Street, Homerton E.9.

Top Row (standing): J. BENNET   W. ANDERSON   E. DARNELL.   S. MEAD   H. RAY.   E. ROBERTSON   T. CLIFT
                    (Committee)   (Treasurer)   (Vice-Captain)   (Committee)   (Committee)

Middle Row (standing): G. F. HARPER   W. CHARGE   G. HARWOOD   H. MEAD.   S. BRETT.   J. J. VYSE   E. A. PRIOR   F. VYSE
                       (Chairman)   (Trainer)   (Captain)   (Hon. Sec.)   (Committee)

Bottom Row (sitting): W. BURGESS.   A. FREE.   H. ODWELL.   B. ANDERSON.   R. LANGDON.

Above: *Stanstead Abbotts Football Club, 1920-21, winners in the East Herts League Division 1, and Finalists in the Rolleston Charity Cup.*

Below: *Stanstead Abbotts Football Team in the late 1950s photographed in Millfield, Cappell Lane, where they beat Allenburys Sports Club 5-0.*

A long-forgotten feature at Great Amwell in the 1930s — 'The Amwell Club' at Concrete Utilities in Lower Road. Above: *the tennis courts with the church in the background.* Below: *The pool, advertised as: 'the most delightful open air swimming pool in England — 100 yds straight swim, 30 yds wide.' With the outbreak of the Second World War, the club closed and its premises were used by the Home Guard as a training-ground. Houses occupy the site today.*

Above: *A Great Amwell tableau in the procession celebrating the coronation of Queen Elizabeth II on 2 June 1953. Many of the children wore coats as it was so cold.*
Below: *A children's coronation tea in the big barn at Sheepcotes Farm, Great Amwell, on 2 June 1953.*

Royal bonfires: (left) at Great Amwell in 1897 for Queen Victoria's Diamond Jubilee; and (right) at Hertford Heath in 1897 for the same event..

EVENTS AND CELEBRATIONS

Celebrations were a social solvent — royal celebrations, in particular, providing opportunities for communities to demonstrate their cohesion and sense of solidarity. They also involved rituals — rituals involving fire, feasts, flags and fun, though the acts of collective worship that often preceded such occasions are not usually photographed.

Photographs give a vivid, if partial, impression of the manner in which the peoples of these villages had fun in times of national celebration. It is perhaps appropriate that Hertford Heath, the site of an Armada beacon of 1588, should be represented among photographs of the beacons that were lit to mark Queen Victoria's Diamond Jubilee of 1897.

Stanstead Abbotts has unusual photographs of the Peace celebrations following the First World War at Bridge Wharf in July 1919 and of the street parties that marked the end of the European War in May 1945. It is a matter of regret that there are no illustrations of the celebrations in these villages of the coronations of Edward VII in 1902 or of George V in 1910, and few illustrations, other than at Hertford Heath, of the Silver Jubilee of King George V in May 1935.

There is more surviving evidence of the carnivals and junketings that marked the Coronation in 1937 of George VI and Queen Elizabeth (now Elizabeth the Queen Mother) in Stanstead Abbotts and Hertford Heath. Great Amwell, on the other hand, has few surviving photographs of coronation celebrations until that of Queen Elizabeth II in 1953.

It is as though the surviving evidence concerning national celebrations fits the social pattern of these villages — plebeian exuberance at Stanstead Abbotts and Hertford Heath, patrician restraint at Great Amwell. But the surviving pattern of photographic evidence is more the result of accident than socially determined.

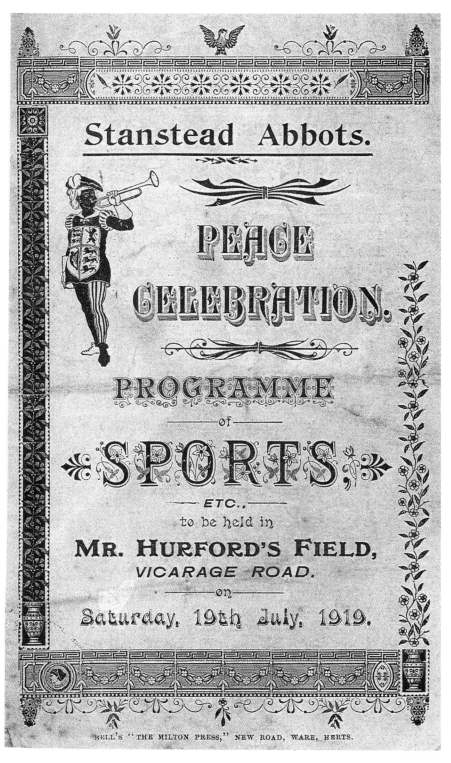

The programme of Peace Celebrations of 19 July 1919 at Stanstead Abbotts. The armistice that brought the First World War to an end was signed on 11 November 1918. The treaty of peace which put a formal end to the war with Germany was signed at Versailles on 28 June 1919. Three weeks later, Stanstead Abbotts celebrated the end to the war in its own style. The programme began with River Sports at 10 am, followed in the afternoon by the Field Sports and a Comic Football Match, with an interval for a Children's Tea. The celebrations were rounded off with a Fireworks Display at dusk at The Potter's Gap.

Two views of the River Sports at Bridge Wharf, Stanstead Abbotts, as part of the Peace Celebrations in July 1919.

Above: *The opening day of Hertford Heath's new village hall on 4 May 1935.   It was built to commemorate the Silver Jubilee of King George V and Queen Mary which was celebrated two days later.   Harry Fitch, son of the hall's builder, still lives in the village.*
Below: *The Coronation dinner for pensioners of Hertford Heath in the Parish Hall, 12 May 1937.*

Above: *Haileybury's contribution to the Hertford Heath carnival to celebrate the Coronation of King George VI and Queen Elizabeth on 12 May 1937.*
Below: *The Coronation celebrations in Hertford Heath also had a traditional flavour.*

Above: *A wartime parade in about 1943 by the Haileybury Officers Training Corps on the village green at Hertford Heath. The donor of this photograph, Mrs Lily Bean, who was to serve for 35 years on the parish council, is standing outside The Goat, accompanied by her two small children.*
Below: *A wartime procession along London Road, Hertford Heath, led by the Women's Section of the British Legion followed by ARP (Air Raid Precautions) wardens and civilians — at some time before 25 July 1944 when the pair of houses on the right were destroyed in a bombing raid.*

Above: *Residents of St. Margarets Road and Stanstead Road celebrate Victory in Europe (VE) Day in May 1945.*

Right: *A children's VE-Day tea party at The Roundings at Hertford Heath.*

Above: *The wedding of Mr and Mrs Gerald Baker in August 1940, with the couple being driven away from St. Andrew's Church by the Stanstead Abbotts Fire Brigade, whose captain Frank Lawrence was the bride's father.*

Below: *'Gifts from Australia' being distributed during the Second World War at the Chapman barn, which was next to the old Fire Station in Stanstead Abbotts and opposite the Parish Hall in Roydon Road. The event was organised by the Red Cross whose local commandant, Mrs. E.T. Pearce, is second from the right. She was the wife of the headmaster of the village school.*

Victory Tea May 9th 1945

Two views of the VE-Day tea party held in South Street, Stanstead Abbotts, to celebrate the end of the Second World War in Europe on 9 May 1945.

Two views of the Festival of Britain celebrations at Stanstead Abbotts in May 1951. Above: *the pageant put on by the Brownies in the garden of Warrax, Cappell Lane.*

Right: *the Festival Queen, Rosemary Morris, with her maids of honour Mary Eva (left) and Phyllis Alban, and two smaller attendants.*

The procession outside St. Margarets Church on 7 June 1948, following the benediction of the Vicarage and the extension of the churchyard by the Bishop of St. Albans, the Right Revd Philip Loyd.

T S Robinson

Camera House
Stanstead Abbotts

In June 1903, Stanstead Abbotts was extensively flooded. On this occasion, however, a professional photographer Thomas Robinson, who had studios in Homerton and Stanstead Abbotts, was on hand to capture these pictures of the flood devastation in the High Street. He was facing west from a point just beyond the corner of Millers Lane (the Oak public house is now the Lord Louis) and both the photographer and his equipment would have been awash. Subjects had to remain motionless for some seconds if the exposure was not to be spoilt.

Stanstead Abbotts High Street awash again, this time in 1928.

FLOOD AND FIRE

The surviving photographic evidence of disasters is largely confined to Stanstead Abbotts. This was understandable in the case of floods because Stanstead Abbotts High Street was built over drained marshlands, and the slightest rise in the water table resulted in the High Street being awash.

One remarkable bonus for this book — though it would have been little consolation for the victims — is that a professional photographer was on hand in Stanstead Abbotts High Street in 1903 to capture the watery devastation on camera.   The photography itself is a technical achievement in the circumstances because the photographer had to operate in flood conditions himself.

No photographer of comparable expertise was on hand to capture the fires that afflicted these communities in the period covered by this book, though there are photographs to document the wreckage that resulted. What is remarkable is not that maltings sometimes caught fire but that, with heat processes so near to construction timbers, they did not catch fire more frequently.

Left: *Yet again ... rescuing operations in the vicinity of Amwell Lane in the floods of March 1947. The Lea Valley suffered devastating floods following a rapid thaw after a very severe winter.*

Below: *And again ... the 1968 floods in Stanstead Abbotts High Street, with Ted Chandler (in white coat) outside his hardware and electrical shop.*

Above: *Ruins of a Stanstead Abbotts maltings which burned down about 1890. Given the heat processes involved, and (to judge from the smouldering embers in this photograph), the quantity of timber used in a malting construction, it is remarkable that fires were not more common.*
Below: *The great St. Margarets rubber-dump blaze of 30 April 1950, reported the next day in the* Daily Graphic: *'The cloud... blocked out a peaceful Sunday afternoon.... It came from a fire among 7000 tons of rubber.... Fireman from 15 brigades fought the blaze. The smoke held up trains on the Liverpool Street-Hertford East line. A watchman found the fire after ordering two boys from the dump.   The fire was under control last night.'*

Great Amwell church choir in 1885 with the vicar, the Revd. Richard Parrott in the centre. The Revd. William Harvey, then curate, is third on the left.

PEOPLE

We come finally to what has made it all possible — the people who lived in these villages and contributed to their social life and ethos.

This section, like all the others, can only be partial and unrepresentative. Inevitably, photographs and portraits chosen for inclusion in this section are of the unusual or the exceptional or even the eccentric. The typical villager appears in preceding sections. Among the sea of faces that look out from these photographs, only one or two can now be identified. No matter. Their contributions are no less important for being anonymous.

Opposite (top): Robert Mylne, who, as Chief Engineer to the New River Company, began the long association of the Mylne family with Great Amwell. A Scotsman of a quarrelsome disposition (an employee found him 'as hot as pepper and as proud as Lucifer') but with an international reputation as an architect, he built the first Blackfriars Bridge in 1770. He was also consultant architect to the Dean and Chapter of St. Paul's Cathedral. When he died in 1811 he was not buried in the family tomb at Great Amwell which he built, but in the vault of St. Paul's, close to the tomb of Sir Christopher Wren whose famous epitaph ('if you seek a monument, look around') he devised.

Opposite (bottom): William Chadwell Mylne succeeded his father, Robert, as Engineer to the New River Company. Following the enclosure of the Great Amwell common fields in 1837, he bought a considerable quantity of land and became a major landowner in the parish. He lived in various houses in Great Amwell, including River Cottage and Amwell Grove, before building Lea Court (now the Flint House) for his asthmatic wife between 1842 and 1845. He died there in 1863.

Above: *Afternoon Tea at The Firs, in Pepper Hill, Great Amwell, c.1895. George Chaplin had five sons and five daughters — three of whom are seen here with their mother and nephew.*
Below, left: *The Revd. William J. Harvey, curate of Great Amwell from 1884 to 1893, and then vicar from 1893 to 1938. He was also incumbent of St. Margarets from 1905. His wife Jessie, the younger daughter of Richard Parrott, inherited the patronage of the living of Great Amwell from her mother Harriet. William Harvey was also editor of* The Anglo-Catholic.
Below, right: *The patriarchal figure of Frederick Parker of Glebe Cottages, Great Amwell. He had been the parish clerk for 50 years when this photograph was taken in about 1920.*

Above: *The Wilkins family pose outside Glebe Cottages, Great Amwell, for a family portrait in 1906. In the background between the two elder sons can be seen the tall chimney of Amwell Marsh pumping station, erected in 1883. Harriet, seen here on the left, was later to be the wife of Thomas Knight, the printer of Hoddesdon.*

Below: *Ted Wilkins and Ned Dewberry proudly display their new motor bikes outside Glebe Cottages in Great Amwell in 1906. Edward Dewberry later succeeded his father-in-law, Frederick Parker (pictured opposite) as parish clerk.*

Above: *Sitting in the stocks for fun at Great Amwell in about 1894. One of these men, however, was the last to sit in the stocks for real. The stocks were later moved from behind the George The Fourth to their present position in the churchyard.*

Below: *Labourers sitting drinking on a bench outside The Goat public house, Hertford Heath, at some time in the later 1920s.*

Above: *The St. Margarets Baden Powell Girl Guides in about 1912. Baden Powell founded the Guides in 1910. This is one of the earliest photographs of any local company. It was formed by two sisters from Stanstead Abbotts, Edith and Annie Clift. Edith Clift, standing to the left of the Revd. William Farmer of Ware, was an infants' teacher at Stanstead Abbotts school and appears in school photographs like the one on p.126. Both sisters lived all their lives in the village.* Below: *The Stantstead Abbotts Cubs in the 1950s with the Scout leaders, including Cecil 'Skip' Hitch, on left of the back row.*

Left: *Edward and Agatha Barlow on the occasion of their Golden Wedding in September 1940. He was chairman of Stanstead Abbotts Parish Council and his wife a member of the Women's Institute. They had lived at Warrax since 1901.*

Below: *Two well-known figures in Stanstead Abbotts — Gert and Nell Springham. They were photographed outside the narrow jettied house next to the Red Lion, where with their brother, Bob, they kept a fruit and vegetable shop.*

Above: *The congregation and friends of the Countess of Huntingdon's (Congregational) Chapel in Cappell Lane, Stanstead Abbotts, at an anniversary dinner held in July 1981. The minister, Mr. S.C. Smith, and his wife are seated, third and fourth from the left. The photograph includes many people still living in the village.*

Below: *Ted Chandler receiving a certificate for the best-kept garden in the Ashlea Room in Stanstead Abbotts. As well as gardening, his great interest was in the history of the village and many of the old photographs he collected are reproduced in this book. After selling his shop in the High Street, Ted became Head of Make-up at the BBC and later an extra in many TV films.*

Above: *The Stanstead Abbotts Evergreen Club choir, winners in April 1981 of the Hertford Cup awarded by the Hertfordshire Old People's Welfare Council, at the Castle Hall, Hertford. Their conductor, Betty Sewell, receives the cup and certificate while choir members look on. Sam Newman, many of whose pictures appear in this book, is fifth from the left at the back (Copyright: Hertfordshire Mercury).*

Below: *The 'King's Messengers' of St. Margarets church, with the vicar, the Revd. Young, in the 1940s.*

Two views of the legendary Arthur ('Archie') Miller of Riverside, Stanstead Abbotts. He was reputed to be England's champion otter-catcher — an occupation which was intended to protect the Amwell Magna Fishery. When the top photograph (right) was taken in 1951, he claimed that at Easneye he had caught his 87th otter. Otters became extinct in Hertfordshire in 1978, but were reintroduced into the Amwell Quarry Wildlife Area in 1991.

Below: *Archie Miller achieved national fame in 1937 when he was photographed by The* Daily Mirror *sitting up in a coffin, which he used as a bed. He died in 1959.*

Above: *Stanstead Abbotts Home Guard, No 1 Platoon, 1942. Jim Newman, who was born in Stanstead Abbotts 87 years ago and now lives on the Folly Estate, is on the right of the middle row.*
Below: *Claude Jupp and his son Ronald together at French and Jupp's in about 1950. Claude, on the left, was an Olympic sprinter in 1896. Many of his records were unbeaten 50 years later.*

Index